I was Prompted to Write These Stories

Donald Marino

Contents

Chapter		
1	Coming Home	1
2	Spector	7
3	Cart	11
4	Desert	17
5	I thought I saw	21
6	Omnipotent	25
7	Alone with everyone	29
8	Spring	33
9	The Force	37
10	The grass is always greener	43
11	The Thing	49
12	Airplane	53
13	Italian Restaurant	57
14	Baseball Field	63
15	First Snow Fall	69

16 Ten Dollar Bill **73**

17 Faded Photograph **79**

18 Ghoast **85**

19 Blue Sky **91**

20 Central Park **97**

21 About the Author **103**

I WAS PROMPTED TO WRITE THESE STORIES
A BOOK OF SHORT STORIES
By Donald L. Marino

This book is based on prompts. The first eleven prompts came from my friends Rob, Sid and Jim. Every week over the winter one of us would give a prompt. We would all write a story, and send them to each other. Once a week we had a group phone call and talked about the stories. Then then next person would give their prompt. These are my stories from those prompts.

The last nine prompts I ask my good friend Mary Jean to give me prompts so I would have twenty stories for this book.

I want to thank all my friends for the prompts.

I was Prompted to Write These Stories

Copyright © 2024 by Donald Marino
All rights reserved. No part of this book may be reproduced in any manner whatsoever without written permission except in the case of brief quotations embodied in critical articles and reviews.
First Printing, 2024

{ 1 }

Coming Home

A big burly man, with reddish brown hair and beard walked into a Love's service station near the Florida, Georgia line. He walked into the dining area and sat at the bar.

"Well, hey Ben, how you doing?" A waitress walked over to him.

"Well Amy, there is a short in my fuse box and it keeps blowing fuses in my truck, and I had to order the part. So, I'm staying here till it comes." Ben shook his head frustrated.

"Well, it could be worse." She pointed to a young man sitting in the corner booth.

Ben took a long look. He had strawberry blond hair, and looked like he must work out. He looked a mess at the moment, but he guessed that wasn't his usual state.

"He came out to his parents and his dad kicked him out. He was sleeping under the picnic table outside this morning."

"Really?"

"We have had many talks you and me. I know you went through almost the same thing." Amy looked at him and sighed.

Ben smiled, he had a big smile that lit up a room and made you feel warm all over. "I'll go talk to him."

"You want your usual?" Amy smiled at him.

"Get us both a BLT, me a black coffee and him a soda." Ben stood and headed toward the table. Ben was only Twenty-eight but carried himself like a much older man.

"I'm so glad you dropped by today." Amy smiled and headed toward the kitchen.

"Can I join you?" Ben asked as he approached the table.

The young man looked up, you could tell he had been crying, his eyes were all puffy and red.

"Yeah, I guess." He sat up straight.

"I'm Ben, what's your name?" Ben reached out his hand as he sat down.

"Trent." He shook Ben's hand in return.

"Well nice to meet you." Ben smiled his big smile again.

"Did I do something wrong?" Trent asked not sure why this guy was talking to him.

"Here we go boys eat up." Amy was there with the food and a big smile of her own.

"Oh, I didn't order anything. I don't have any money." Trent said pushing the BLT aside.

"Oh, honey Ben here got if for you. He is a real sweetie; I've known him for a long time now." Amy turned and smiled at Ben as she walked away.

Trent was totally confused, but grabbed the sandwich as he was starving.

"So, the word is you came out and your family didn't handle it well." Ben started as he took a bite of his sandwich.

"Didn't handle it well is an understatement. My dad cut me off totally. No college this fall, no phone, no home, nothing. Said if I was going to be a godless piece of shit then I was dead to him." Trent said as the tears started in his eyes again.

"I'm sorry to hear that, my family was kind of like that, but I was already on my own when I came out. Most of my family still won't talk to me." Ben took another bite of his sandwich as he finished.

"Really?" Trent was surprised.

"Ask Amy, she knows." Ben pointed to the waitress who only smiled and nodded.

"Well, I don't know what to do. No one will help me fearing my dad's reaction. I turn 19 in a month and I'm all alone."

"Well, I am stuck here for three days at least. My rig needs a part that I had to order. I'm staying at the budget inn across the street. You can share the room and we will figure out how to help you." Ben offered.

"Really? Why would you help me?" Trent was shocked at the offer.

"Because I know how it feels to have no one. It's not a good feeling." Ben smiled at him.

Trent looked over at Amy who just smiled and nodded yes to him.

"OK." Trent finished his sandwich and the two said see you later to Amy and they went over to the hotel. The two spent the afternoon talking and Trent relaxed. Ben could see the tension evaporate as evening drew near. Ben ordered a pizza for them and they sat and watched tv and ate. Trent took a shower then crawled into the king size bed.

"Sorry, there is only one bed, but I wasn't expecting company." Ben had said to him.

"It's fine I don't take up much space." Trent had said and he laid close to the edge of the bed as he could.

Ben got a shower and got into the other side of the bed. Trent could smell his fresh showered body and the smell intoxicated him.

The next day they were at the diner for breakfast when Amy came to work.

"Well boys how did it go?"

"He is right everyone is afraid of his father. Most just hung up on him."

"Ben said we can look for shelters today."

"After you help me clean my truck. You promised." Ben laughed and his smile lit things up as usual.

"I know." Trent smiled back. He liked how Ben's energy made him feel.

Later when Amy took a break and stepped outside, she watched as the two of them were washing the rig and spraying each other. She smiled.

"Funny how things seem to work themselves out." She said to herself.

That afternoon calls when as bad as the day before calls. No local shelter could help him.

Trent lay on the bed in a heap, and Ben looked at him. He had no idea how to help him.

"I'm going for a coffee across the street. You want anything?" Ben asked

"No." Trent softly replied.

Ben walked into the truck stop, as Amy was just leaving work.

"Long shift today?" Ben smiled at her.

"How are things going?" Amy smiled at him.

"Not good, can't find any help for him."

"You know you two looked happy today."

"What?" Ben tried to play stupid.

"Don't play dumb, I know you to well."

"Ok Yes he is my type, but."

"But what?"

"But he has just come out. He needs time."

"Time for?"

"Oh, I don't know, you ask to many questions."

"Ok, you have been alone for how long. He has nowhere to go, if nothing else.."

"I'm not looking for if nothing else." Ben stormed off "I'm going for coffee then back to my room." He muttered.

Amy said nothing knowing she was right was all she needed.

That night after Ben took his shower he stood and looked at Trent laying there in bed. Trent had moved closed to the middle of the bed. That made Ben smile but he still crawled in on his own side. He laid on his side just watching Trent breathe.

Trent could smell his fresh body again and it was driving him crazy. The aroma was more than he could take and he found himself sliding back so that his back was up against Ben's chest. He tried to make it seem like he was doing this in his sleep, and now he could feel his beard barely touch his neck and Ben's breath on his ears. He felt electric run though his whole body. He wasn't sure if he should run or stay. Suddenly Ben rested his head just so his chin was touching his shoulder. Before he realized what he was doing Trent reached back and pulled Ben's arm around him, and they both drifted off to sleep.

When Trent woke in the morning Ben was already up drinking a coffee.

"Good morning." Trent said without looking at him.

"Good morning. My part came so I will be heading out today." Ben said

"Oh." Trent wasn't sure what to say.

"I uh..."

"I'm sorry about last night." Trent interrupted him.

"What?"

"I'm sorry, I shouldn't have done that."

"Listen I like you and I enjoyed holding you."

"Really?"

"Yes, after talking to Amy again this morning she thinks, well I mean I would like it if you would come with me."

"Really."

"We could see if this would work. You and me I mean."

"I would like that."

"We can take it slow."

Trent jumped and hugged him. The two got their things together. As the Rig was getting fixed the two went for breakfast.

"I take it we are..." Amy smiled at them.

"Got to take it slow and see where it goes." Ben said with a big smiled that was mirrored by Trent.

The two spent the next several months becoming closer and more in love. Trent had started calling him Daddy, which Ben liked and he called Trent his boy. They traveled up and down the east coast. Then one day in late October when they were on an interstate in the north east, a snow squaw came out of nowhere. All Trent heard was squealing tires and breaking glass. Ben yelling get down as two by fours came flying out of nowhere, then there was quiet.

"Daddy are you ok?" Trent looked up and realized he was covered in blood. To his horror two of the two by fours had hit Ben one in the head and one in the shoulder. Things seemed scrambled after that. Someone had drug him out of the truck as he screamed "No." Then next thing he knew he was sitting in a police station.

"Your parents have been looking for you for months now." The officer was telling him. "Your dad is on the phone." The officer pushed the speaker button.

"Son don't worry we are coming for you." His dad said.

Everything seemed a blur. He saw the cops taking his bulletproof vest off and belt with his cuffs etc. And hang them on the back of the chair in front of him. Said something about his blood-soaked clothes and a thirty-car pileup. His dad was on the phone saying "Don't worry son we found a place that will help you to stop being gay." Memories of ben flooded his head and then pictures of Ben's lifeless body lying there. He looked down at his blood soak clothes.

"Daddy I'm coming home." Trent yelled as he moved.

"Yes, son you are." His dad replied as Trent retrieved the gun from the officer's belt that hung on the chair. He put the gun in his mouth and pulled the trigger as everyone in the station yelled "No" and tried to stop him but it was too late, the gun went off and silence filled the room as Trent lay dead on the floor.

"Hello, what's going on?" His father finally said.

{ 2 }

Spector

"More strange crafts have shown up in the sky." A news announcer came over the short-wave radio that Dale and his family were listening to as they huddled deep in an abandon coal mine.

Dale had moved his family here several weeks ago when the first UFO's showed up. The military had gone after them but were shot down easily. They didn't make any contact just hovered there, and now more were showing up. There were a couple of other families in the mine as well and they took turns going out to look for food and supplies.

"Dale honey." A pretty young lady who now had tears running over the dust and dirt that covered her face, said as she came up beside him.

"Yes." Dale couldn't even look at her.

"What do you think is going to happen?" She asked trying to stop her tears.

"I don't know." Dale said as the voice came back on the radio.

"This is the worst specter we could have imagined." The announcer said with fear in his voice. "Pyramids all over the planet are lighting up, even in places we never knew they existed." The announcer voice when quiet and you could hear him sob softly.

"Dale we should make one last run." A man said as he came up beside him. He was fighting back tears.

"I don't think we are going to need." Dale was barely able to say.

"The UN has decided to bomb the pyramids with nuclear war heads." The voice came again on the radio.

"Maybe you're right, we don't need the run." The other man fell back with his head in his hand tears freely flowing.

Dale moved over toward his two daughters who were sitting a short distance away and his wife followed.

"Daddy when can we go home?" The oldest who was only six years old asked.

"Soon honey, soon." Dale said trying to keep things calm when on the inside he was full of fear and despair. He had always been able to protect his family and now there is nothing he could do, but he had decided days ago that he couldn't let his family see him be weak.

"Let's get some sleep." His wife said to the girls as she snuggled up beside them.

The night drug slowly on as the minutes passed by with only the sound of water dripping from the ceiling. Dale kept looking out into the dark waiting for the end to come, however that might be. He hoped it would be fast he did not want to see his family suffer. They lived in coal country in north east Pennsylvanian, not too far from the Berwick nuclear plant. For sure that would be something the ships would take out.

"It's morning." The man from last night said to Dale who had just fallen asleep.

Dale opened his eyes surprised to be doing so.

"What do you think happened." The man asked.

"Don't know." Dale moved to the radio and turned it on.

"all of them. Not one of the bombs hit their targets." The announcer was saying.

Dale and the other man just looked at each other in disbelief.

"Armies around the world have been wiped out by what can only be described as laser beams." The announcer continued. "Reports are millions have been, for lack of a better work, burned alive." The announcer went quiet for a minute. "The end is here folks. May God have mercy on us."

Dale shut off the radio.

"What do we do?" The other man asked.

Dale ran his hand through his dirty hair and shook his head.

"We go for supplies." Dale sighed not sure that was the best idea, but he needed to do something useful.

A short time later the two men were making their way back into town. Dale looked at the park. Pictures of his girls playing on the swings flashed through his mind and now the park had no life at all. They crawled through the broken glass doors on the grocery store and pictures of him and his girls shopping flashed through his mind. They would always want cookies and usually he would give in. Now there wasn't a cookie to be had. They found a few can goods that had rolled under some shelves. They left and headed toward the dollar store, and more pictures of his kids and wife went through his mind when times were better, and seeing things now was almost too much. It looked like a ghost town. Homes and stores were broken into and anything worth taken was gone. They searched the dollar store and found nothing. They saw some others coming to do the same thing and made sure to avoid them, they had a few things and didn't want them stolen. Then they slowly made their way back to the mine.

"Did you find anything?" Dale's wife asked

"A few things, but there is not much out there anymore." Dale sighed as they suddenly felt a rumble under their feet.

Dale grabbed the radio and turn it on and the rumbling came again.

"The pyramids have all started shooting beams of energy into the air." The announcer was almost yelling in shock. The rumbling came under their feet again. "The ships seem to be getting charged from them." The announcer continued in the shocked voice.

"What do you thing is happening?" Dale's wife asked.

Dale said nothing just looked in shock at the radio.

"The pyramids are so bright with a blue light and shaking violently, it's seemed they may explode……" The announcer's voice was gone, just static.

The rumbling came again and harder this time.

"We need to get out of here. This is going to collapse." Dale said and pushed his family in front of him, followed by the other two families. They rushed out into the day light which for the most of them hurt their eyes as they had not been out of the mine in weeks.

"Oh my God!" Screamed Dale's wife as she pointed. A large ship moved over head toward the power plant. The ground shook again and they all fell. Dale turned in time to see the coal mine collapse. He turned back to get to his wife and children as the ship shot a blue beam at the power plant. The ground shook once again and Dale started to cry out to his wife and children to come to him, although he had no idea what to do. Dale looked up in time to see a blue explosion fly across the valley killing everything in its path.

{ 3 }

Cart

Skyler Walker was in the waiting room of an attorney's office. Not just any office one of the best in the city. Certainly no one he knew could afford this guy, but here he sat at two thirty on a Friday afternoon. He had gotten a certified letter that he was to be here for the reading of the will of Benjamin Ulysses Dent the third. He had no idea who this was or why he would be in the will. He looked around and no one else was showing up. He had hoped to listen in on the others talking so he would have some idea who this was.

He looked down at himself. He had just come from work. He was a foreman for a construction company. They had been building a house and he was cover in saw dust. He had tried to brush it off. He had planned on going home first to shower, but that didn't happen now he looked like a bum. His dark brown hair and beard looked like it had blond high lights from the dust.

"Ah Mr. Walker please come in." The attorney said as he stood in the opened door way to his office.

Skyler looked up his brown eyes were even highlighted in dust. He went into the office and sat where the attorney had pointed for him to sit.

"I'm sorry for the way I look. I just came from work." Skyler started.

"It's fine." The attorney smiled at him.

"I'm not sure you have the right guy." Skyler was feeling a little uncomfortable.

"Oh, I have the right guy. You may not recognize the name because you called him by a different name."

"Oh, what did I call him?"

"Buddy." The attorney waited a minute for it to sink in.

"You mean homeless buddy with the cart?"

"Yes."

"I just had a coffee with him last week."

"He passed the next day I believe."

"Wait this doesn't make sense. He had no money..."

"Let me explain. Do you know his back story at all?"

"Some."

"At nineteen his parents, who owned a lawn care service were killed by an employee. The employee was on drugs and his parents had tried to help him, but he fell off the wagon and killed them when they refused to give him money for drugs. This disturbed him so much he said he never wanted to have anything worth killing for, so he became homeless and distrusting of people."

"OK."

"This letter will explain the rest." The attorney handed him a sealed envelope with his name on it.

He opened it slowly and began to read.

Skyler my friend;

If you are reading this then it means I have passed, but I want you
To know your simple acks of kindness over the years have meant
More than you will ever know. I have left everything I own to you.
Please follow my attorney's instructions on what to do next. My
Friend you and you alone put a spark of hope in my life that there
Is good out there. So please enjoy what I left for you.

Your homeless friend
Buddy

"I really don't want anything from him. He had nothing other than that cart full of stuff."

"Here are your instructions." The attorney handed him a bank book. "You are to take the money in the account pay off your house and any bills you have then take your family on a nice vacation."

"What? How much could there be?" Skyler stopped talking when he saw the balance of five point five million dollars. "This can't be right."

"His parents had very large insurance policies and because he was homeless with no real bills, he barely touched it over the years." Next, he handed him two keys. "One is for a safe deposit box at community bank, and the other is for locker twenty-nine at the y where he would go to get showers. and finally here is a journal." He handed him a beat-up hard cover journal.

"His cart is being delivered to your house shortly. In the cart, safety deposit box and locker you will find items that have dates on them. Find that date in the book and it will help you understand why he left you what he did. He said please enjoy life you deserve it."

"That's it?"

"Afraid so. He had strong feelings for you. Always remember it's the little things that you do that mean the most. Now go do as he asked."

The attorney showed him to the door, as he drove home, he couldn't believe what was happening. As he pulled into his driveway a box truck was dropping off the cart that was buddy's.

"What's going on?" His wife asked as she walked up to the truck as he parked.

He explained everything to her and she was as stunned as he was.

"Why don't we just read the journal?"

"Because that isn't what he asked me to do. Let's look through the cart and see what we find. Where are the kids?"

"At mom's swimming. I told her we would be over later."

"OK good."

They both stood and looked at the cart. "I guess we just start pulling stuff out." Skyler Pulled an old blanket off the top. "Wow this is so old It's falling apart."

"Wait, there on the tag a date." His wife pointed, and he looked. September 12, 1976

"Look in the journal." His wife said.

Skyler opened the journal and it was the first entry.

September 12, 1976 A little boy named Skyler gave me a blanket today. After a day of teenagers and adults saying horrible things to me. This little boy said. It's going to be cold Mr. you better cover up.

"I remember that. Mom and I saw a man yell mean things to him. I asked why he would to that. Mom said that you should always show kindness you never know when you may need the same kindness. We went into the five and dime and I saw this blanket. I use my allowance and got it for him. I can't believe he still had this."

"What else is in the cart?" His wife asked.

A tear was in the corner of his eye and he pulled a few odd and ends out and then there was a torn and beat up kite. He remembered it right away but looked for the date. May 11 1979 is what he found, and he went to the journal.

May 11 1979 Skyler and his mom were walking in the park with a kite and Skyler asked his mom if I could help him fly it. His mom looked at me and I said I would be happy to. We flew that kite for an hour or more till it got stuck in the tree. This boy may give me faith in mankind yet.

"I remember that, I got this at the James Way. It was from last year and was on sale. Mom was pregnant with Hunter and due any day, but agree to take me to the park to try and fly it. Dad drove truck and was on the road all the time. I had such a good time that day."

His wife hugged him.

"I can't believe all of this."

"Look, on the bottom of that dairy queen cup there is a date." July 3, 1979

July 3, 1979 Skyler was back today with two ice creams. We sat on the park bench and ate ice cream and talked about what we thought the clouds looked like.

"I am ...." He couldn't say anything else.

He continued to go through the cart and item after item date after date took him back in time and, he teared up more and more.

That Monday he went to the bank and in the Safety deposit box there were old coins and silver and gold pieces, but there was one fifty cent coin in a plastic case with the date. August 17 1977.

August 17 1977 Skyler stopped by and gave me a fifty-cent piece and said he was told it was good luck. He hoped I had good luck finding a home.

Skyler remembered it. His uncle had given that to him and said it was good luck. He remembered thinking he knew who needed good luck the most and gave it to buddy.

He went to the Y and in the locker, he found a pair of new shoes in a box dated October 22 1986. He couldn't believe what he was seeing. He opened the Journal

October 22 1986 Skyler came by today. He is getting so big. He is working now and bought me a new pair of shoes. He gives me hope when every one else is so mean and thoughtless. I don't think I can ever wear these.

Skyler took the shoes out and just held them and tears rolled. He had thought buddy had sold or given the shoes away. Then he heard a thud on the floor and there was a base ball on the floor dated. May 30 1984. His eyes got wide he knew exactly what that was. He looked in the journal.

May 30 1984 today thugs tried to rob me, but God sent my guardian angel, Skyler, He was walking home from playing baseball and saw what was going on. He threw the baseball, a wicked fast pitch, and nailed one of the thugs in the back who fell to the ground.

The other two turned to see him running at them swinging a bat. They ran and left their friend who slowly got going himself.

"Oh my god. I never realized how much these little things meant to him. Rest in peace my friend I will miss you. I am so glad I was there for you."

{ 4 }

Desert

"Honey I am so glad to be home that was a long flight." Jenny said as she fell into the couch her long blond hair a mess from being on the go for over twenty-four hours, her pretty blue eyes had huge bags underneath them.

"Me to. I loved Egypt, trip of a life time, but man I'm beat." Mike said as he closed the front door to their New Jersey bi-level home.

"I'm getting a shower. I'll unpack everything later." Jenny pushed herself up off the couch.

"Look what I got." Mike smiled. He pulled out a small gold coin.

"You brought that home?" Jenny almost yelled.

"Yes, of course. It was just lying there in the sand."

"Are you crazy you know what that tour guide said about treasure in that area. It all has a curse on it."

"Oh, come on you don't believe in that."

"I do." She looked up. "I have nothing to do with this." She spit in the air several times.

"What was that supposed to do?"

"Protect me from whatever you brought home."

"It's just a silly piece of gold. It's nothing."

"I'm going for a shower. I don't want to see that when I come back down."

Jenny went upstairs.

"It's nothing." He yelled after her.

He went into the kitchen tossed the gold onto the island and got a drink and sat on a bar stool and picked up the gold piece. He flipped it around and saw that there were some kinds of markings, but nothing he could make out. He spun it on the counter a little and watched it wabble and fall on the counter.

"It's just a stupid piece of gold." He got up and walked into the living room and turned on the TV. He was watching tv and felt something rush by his head. He jumped as he was half asleep and looked around and saw nothing.

"Must have been a bug." He looked back at the tv and the gold piece was on the coffee table. Mike jumped up.

"I left that on the counter." He looked around for a few minutes, and realized he was alone. "I must have brought it in here. I'm tired and just don't remember."

He sat back down and started watching tv again. Then the tv went out, nothing but a humming noise.

"This tv is only a couple of months old." He was messing with the remote.

"You took it." A low voice said as it rushed by his ear.

"who's there?" Mike was on his feet again. He spun around looking in all directions.

"Why?" The voice raced by him again.

"I didn't take anything." Mike was desperately looking for something to defend himself with.

"It was mine." The voice was loud now and Mike started to sweat.

"I'm sorry."

"You will be." The voice was harsh again. And Mike was hit in the chest, like a canon had been shot at him, he flew backwards into the kitchen.

"I'll put it back." Mike barely was able to get out, as he got to his feet.

"To late." The voice came again. Mike saw knives come out of the block they were stored in, and come straight at him.

"No." Mike yelled as he tried to dodge them, but he was to late they pierced his chest in several places, blood flowed freely and there was a stream of blood running through the grooves of the tile.

"You must pay for your treachery." The voice came again.

"I'm sorry." Mike said as blood was now coming out of his mouth and adding to the growing river on the floor.

One of the heavy wooden chairs that sat at the kitchen table went up into the air and came down hard one leg through his heart and one through his skull.

Jenny was done taking a shower and walked into the hall way she heard the tv.

"Oh god a stupid western again. I'm way too tired for that." Jenny walked into the bed room and felt something brush her shoulder. She turned quickly and saw no one. Her heart was racing.

"Hey honey you down there?" She asked but no response came. "He must have fallen asleep watching tv. I'm to tired to fight with him." She waved her hand and headed into the bedroom again.

"Why?" She heard a low voice whisper in her ear. She turned quickly again her heart almost pounding out of her chest now. The bedroom door slammed shut.

"Mike!" she screamed as she raced to the door and grabbed the door knob, but something or someone grabbed her hair and pulled so hard she flew backwards across the room landing against the dresser. Clumps of her hair had been pulled out and now lay on the floor, blood trickled down her face and neck.

"I didn't do it!" She screamed knowing it was something attached to the gold coin.

"You didn't stop him." She felt something grab her throat and she was being pushed to the wall then up the wall. She screamed kicking her feet.

"That was mine and you took it." The voice came again.

"I didn't take. Mike." She stopped talking realizing Mike didn't answer because he was asleep, he was dead, and she was next. She started crying trying to fight free.

"You must pay for your treachery." She was fighting for what little air she could get now, and blood started to come from her mouth. She was lifted and slammed down over the bed post. Through the middle of her back and out the front. Blood flowed down over her like lava out of a volcano and onto the perfectly made bed. And silence took over the house.

The next day Their friends had shown up to see the horrifying scene and called 911. The cops were questioning them as the EMTs were taking the bodies out. The cops couldn't get over how violent everything was. Two EMTs were taking Mike's body out when the one spotted the Gold Coin. No one was looking so he picked it up and put it in his pocket.

"No one will miss it." He said to himself.

{ 5 }

I thought I saw

Bruce sat staring at pictures from another folder from a case he had years ago. He was retired now but he used to be Detective Bruce Santone. He currently was going through old cases, trying to figure out who he saw a couple days before. He was sure this person was dead. He was in a market walking down the candy isle not paying attention to where he was going, more intent on what candy he wanted and he bumped into a guy. He looked up to say excuse me and the man looked shocked, hiding his face and quickly went on his way without saying a word.

His daughter had begged him to update all his files on a laptop, but he was having none of that. The old way was always better. He sat at his kitchen table smoking a cigar, which his daughter hated. And looking at old photos.

"That's him." He pointed to a picture of a man in his late twenty's. "But he was killed." He ran his hand with the cigar in it through his thinning hair.

"Dad dinner is ready." His daughter yelled from the kitchen. She had moved in with him after his wife had passed away two years ago.

"OK, I'll be out in a minute." They always sat at a smaller table in the kitchen to eat. No need to drag everything into the dining room.

The next morning, he grabbed the picture and headed back to the market where he had seen the man in the picture. He was sure it couldn't have been him, but if it was, a man was on death row for something he didn't do.

Bruce sat in his 1970 blue Chevy Impala. His daughter had wanted him to trade it in on a Nissan. "You must be crazy." He had told her. Ok sure the 8-track player didn't work at all but the radio was good. The car itself was still as solid as ever. He had rolled the window down a crack so his cigar smoke would leave the car. His coffee was in the plastic cup holder that hung on the door. He looked across the bench seat to the bag of candy that he had bought the other day at this market, then down to his belly. He had put on some pounds in ten years.

After eating several circus peanuts the man he was looking for walked out of the store. He held up the picture.

"It's him." He laid the picture back down and watched to see where the man went. He got into a small blue escort. Bruce waited for him to pull out and followed at a distance.

"He has some questions to answer." Bruce said to himself.

It was a short drive as the escort parked by some run-down row homes. Bruce turned on the old real to real recorder that would record everything from the wire he was wearing. He got out patting old Betsy on his side, that is what he called his police issued colt.

As the man walked under an overpass Bruce walked up behind him.

"Joe." Bruce yelled out and the man stopped walking for a moment but didn't look back, and then continued walking.

"Joe Ferella." Bruce yelled this time. Once again, the man stopped walking for a moment and then started walking again.

"I know it's you. You have some explaining to do." Bruce yelled now.

The man turned and looked at him. "Detective Santone, how nice to see you." Joe sneered.

"You are supposed to be dead." Bruce raised an eyebrow.

"Yes, and I'm planning on staying that way."

"You know that can't happen." Bruce put his hand by his gun.

"You're retired now, go home and rest."

"I would but there is a man on death row for something he didn't do. And who was in the car that exploded. The DNA was a match to you?"

"Funny story, remember my twin that died at birth, well he didn't die the hospital sold him to a couple on the black market and just told my parents he died. He shows up at my house saying he wants half of what my parents took a life time to build. My parents not his." Joe was yelling now.

"So, he was in the car when it exploded." Bruce shook his head.

"Very good."

"So, the Lewis's were after you and got him?" Bruce asked. "So why not come forward.

"You're not as sharp as you used to be are you." Joe mocked him. "I rigged the car and told him to take if for a drive."

"You framed the Lewis family for it because they were cutting in on your routes." Bruce finished.

"Very good. My Parents spent their whole lives building that business, from a small garden to supplying the tri state area with produce, and the Lewis family was going to come and steel our customers with their inferior products. So, I killed my brother and got rid of the Lewis family. Two birds with one stone."

"But what was the end game for you. You didn't want to live like this." Bruce points around.

"I was going to get my wife and son and go south, have her run the company from Mexico, but you got worried she would be a target and put her in a witness protection program. She sold the company, which I am still mad about. Now I don't even know where she is and the Lewis family has everything."

"That back fired I'd say."

Joe reached behind his back and Bruce pulled his gun.

"That wouldn't be a smart idea." Bruce motioned from him to put up his hands.

"You are retired you can't arrest me. It would be your word against mine anyway."

"I am taking you in one way or another. You killed a man and a man is on death row for something he didn't do. It's time the truth be told. This wire that I am wearing will tell the truth." Bruce smiled at him

Joe hadn't moved his hand and tried to pull his gun and Bruce shot him.

Bruce walked over as Joe rolled on the ground holding his knee that Bruce had shot.

"I told you I was taking you in." Bruce rolled him over and handcuffed him, then called for help.

{ 6 }

Omnipotent

Rob woke in a strange place he had never been before. He was in a huge hall; it was beautiful like something out of Egyptian times. Looking around he saw a gold pen standing upright in a pen stand. He walked to it and looked at it for a few minutes. He looked around and no one was anywhere to be seen. He looked back at the pen. It was the most beautiful pen he had ever seen. The gold sparkled so brightly it was hard to look at but at the same time you didn't want to stop looking at it. He reached out and touched it, then pulled back quickly.

"Anyone here?" His voice echoed throughout the hall, but no one answered back. He started to walk through the hall but kept looking back at the pen. It was to much for him to resist. He ran back and grabbed the pen. It easily came out of the stand and he was shocked at how light it was in his hand.

In seconds however he wasn't sure he had done the right thing. There were loud sounds and things seemed to swirl around him. He felt energy surge through him. He thought to put the pen back but the stand was gone. He tried to just drop the pen, but his hand wouldn't let it go.

Then all the noise stopped. He looked around where the stand once stood now sat a throne and surrounding him were hundreds of what looked like Egyptian soldiers.

"You can have the pen back. I was just looking at it." He extended his arm with the pen in it and ink flowed from it and wrote in the air.

I am Rob keeper of the pen

All the soldiers around him said. "Hail Omnipotent Rob keeper of the pen master of words."

Rob looked confused and had no idea what to say.

"Oh, Omnipotent one of the words. Please take a seat on your throne."

"My what? There is a mistake." He said to the man.

"No mistake oh Omnipotent one. You have pulled the pen from it's stand. Only the Omnipotent one of the words could do that. We have been waiting for you for a very long time." The man said as he helped Rob sit in the throne.

"So, what does that mean?" Rob asked unsure what he was to be doing.

"We are here to serve the Omnipotent one." The man bowed.

"Ok?" Rob looked around for a minute. Thinking one of his friends was playing a joke, but this was a huge hall with hundreds of soldiers.

"What would the Omnipotent one desire?" The man asked and bowed again.

"Explain to me what I do with the pen."

"Of course, Omnipotent one. The pen is magic that only you can control. Hold it up like you are writing and what ever you are thinking the pen will write in the air. The pen is so perfect that ever thing it writes will be celebrated as a master piece. Making you the Omnipotent Rob keeper of the pen master of words."

Rob looked at the man for a moment then lifted his hand with the pen in it. Ink started to flow once again and words appeared in the air. Everyone there was so quiet you could have heard a pin drop. When the pen stopped it had written a short horror story that Rob have been mulling over in his mind. It was perfect, he was in disbelief.

Again, all there repeated "Hail Omnipotent Rob keeper of the pen, master of words."

Then there was a flash of light and what looked like a large scroll rolled up and the writing was gone.

"What happen?" Rob asked the man next to him.

"The magic keeps all your writings safe for all time. To recall any work, you just have to write the title with the pen and it will come back."

Rob thought for a minute and remembered another story he was working on. He held the pen up again and the ink flowed. Infront of him again was a perfect story based on his thoughts.

All there once again said. "Hail Omnipotent Rob keeper of the pen, master of words."

Then again it rolled up in a scroll and disappeared. Wondering if it would really work, he held up the pen and wrote the first title and the story reappeared.

All there once again said "Hail Omnipotent Rob keeper of the pen, master of words."

"My writing really is orgasmic." Rob smiled. He continued to write story after story and all were met with the same response. They never seemed to get tired of his stories, in fact the more he wrote the more they seemed to want.

"I'm getting a little hungry and tired." Rob said to the man standing beside him.

"Whatever you wish just write it and it will be done Omnipotent one."

Rob wrote pizza with extra sauce and bed. In an instant he was sitting on the biggest and most beautiful bed he had ever seen. And beside him was a large pizza.

Rob smiled and wrote pizza for everyone. Instantly there was pizza everywhere.

"Thank you, Omnipotent Rob keeper of the pen, master of orgasmic words." And they all eat.

"Why did they add Orgasmic?" Rob looked at the man.

"Because you said it."

Rob lay back smiling at his good luck, then all of the sudden he felt an elbow in his side.

"Wake up you are getting the pizza all over the bed." Julia yelled at him again.

Rob opened his eyes looking around.

"You wanted to watch this Egyptian thing on the history channel."

"Hu what?"

"You fell asleep and knocked the pizza all over the bed." Julia was trying to wipe sauce off of the blanket. "Get extra sauce you said."

"What, oh sorry dear." Rob said as he looked around.

"What are you looking for?" Julia said as she continued to clean the sauce off the bed.

"Nothing." Rob sighed realizing Orgasmic writing was just a dream.

{ 7 }

Alone with everyone

Jackson stood in his tiny bathroom putting after shave on, and looking in the mirror at a man he wished he weren't. His black hair was slicked back and his clothes lay on the single bed that he could see out of the corner of his eye.

"I miss my bed." Jackson muttered to himself, looking down into the sink as he washed the last of the shaving cream down the drain. He dried his hands, took the two steps to his bedroom and picked up his clothes.

"I can't believe I am going to this party. Nineteen forty-seven has to get better." He sighed heavy as he put his trousers on. Jackson grabbed his blue shirt and something fell to the floor. He looked down to see his inhaler. He sighed and tucked his shirt in and thought about how much he hated that inhaler.

Jackson found out when he was young that he had asthma, and it left him out of a lot of things. His best friend Brent played football, but he couldn't because of his asthma. He wanted to play the trumpet but again his asthma. He tried drums, but the marching in the band was too much. He hung around with his friends, but always felt alone as the stories they told he was never part of.

Then in his fourth year of college, World War two broke out. Brent signed up as did his other friends, but again he couldn't go because of his asthma. But he had been learning engineering and soon found himself working for Chrysler. He helped them refit their plants to make supplies for the war effort. So, Jackson felt he was doing his part, and hoped what he was doing would help his friends.

Jackson sat on the bed to put his shoes on, bent over to pick up the inhaler and put it in his pocket.

"Don't want to leave this behind, that cold winter air will surely have me needing this." Jackson said out loud to no one.

Jackson sat motionless as his green eyes told everyone how he was feeling, even though no one was there.

"Look at this place." Jackson said under his breath.

Jackson thought back a year ago after the war ended. Chrysler had said they were eliminating his job, but that they had a job for him on the floor. He would head the maintenance department. Again, his asthma was a problem. Three times in one week they had to call an ambulance for him. They apologized to him, but said he was high risk and let him go. He tried to keep the nice apartment he had downtown but ended up losing everything.

"Talk to your uncle." His mother had told him.

His uncle Walter owned a small department store downtown. He was in his eighties and was starting to lose it.

"No thanks mom." Jackson had said at first, but he was running out of options, so went to see his uncle.

"My boy, they are all stealing from me. I need someone on the inside to catch them." Uncle Walter told him.

"What do you want me to do?" Jackson asked confused.

"I am putting you head of security for the store. Everyone will think I hired you to catch shoplifters, but you are going to spy on all of them. Catch them in the act." Uncle Walter was almost foaming at the mouth now.

"I don't know." Jackson started.

"Don't worry my boy you'll be great. Now remember you can't be friends with any of them. They are all crooks." Uncle Walter warned him.

Jackson had been doing this job now for several months and did manage to catch a few shop lifters, but the employees all seemed loyal to him. When he tried to tell his uncle this, he didn't want to hear it.

"There is a New Year's Eve party that I am giving the employees. I want you to go and listen closely. When people are drunk, they speak the truth. They will tell what they are doing." Uncle Walter said proud of the evil plan he had come up with.

Jackson was dressed and heading out the door. He couldn't afford a cab, and it was going to be a cold walk so he had a scarf wrapped around his face. It was only a couple blocks to the store; the party was in the basement at the department store's restaurant.

Jackson walked as fast as the sidewalk would let him. He reached down and felt the inhaler in his pocket, he hated it, but it also made him feel safe. He entered the store by the back door, making his way down the stairs to the restaurant that had been decorated for the party. Many of the employees were already there and drinking. The radio was playing swing music.

"Someone changed the station from big band." He said softly to no one.

"Hey Jackson, want a drink?" A young lady, who worked in the lingerie department, came up to him.

"No thanks." Jackson put his hand up to push back the bottle of whatever it was she was trying to hand him. His uncle had told him not to drink, and he thought he better listen just in case his uncle would show up.

"Aww come on, you always turn me down. Won't go out to eat or anything." She complained as she pulled the bottle back.

"Leave him alone." A voice came from behind.

Jackson turned to see the middle-aged man who worked in furniture.

"Don't worry Jackson." He said, as he stirred a red drink of some sort with a small straw. "I know what is going on. Your secret is safe with me." He winked at him and walked away.

"Great." Jackson muttered to himself. Jackson was approached by several other employees and turned them all away. He got some food from the small buffet, found a spot in the corner, sat and ate his food alone while everyone was dancing, drinking and having fun. Midnight came and several couples kissed as the new year came in.

"Straight people, am I right?" The man from the furniture department said rolling his eyes as he walked by.

Jackson smiled, once again alone with everyone else enjoying life around him.

{ 8 }

Spring

Jim woke and had no idea where he was. The last thing he could remember was going to bed, but he was not in his house any longer. Looking around he saw a big computer of some sort that covered the wall in front of him and on a small table attached to the computer was a huge red button. Looking around he realized he was in a cage.

"Our hero is trapped once again; will he be able to escape or will the world be taken over by evil." A booming voice came from nowhere.

"Who, said that? I'm not a hero, I'm just Jim." Jim looked around to see where the voice came from.

"I see you woke up from your little nap." An odd-looking man walked in twisting his long black mustache as he laughed. He wore a large hat that was red and purple striped with goggles strapped to it. He had red gloves on and purple long coat and black boots.

"I'm sorry I don't know what you mean." Jim was even more confused now.

"You thought you were going to stop me again. The sleep gas stopped you." Again, he twisted his mustache and laughed. A tan dog that sat at his feet and laughed and oddly human kind of laugh.

"Can you tell me exactly what is going on here?" Jim asked as he looked at the dog.

"You thought you were going to stop me again, but not this time." The odd man replied.

"Again, I don't know who you are."

"Don't play stupid, you know exactly who I am, and what I am planning on doing." The odd man twisted his mustache again and laughed.

"Sorry, you have the wrong guy. Now can I please go home?" Jim tested the bars, and they didn't move very easily.

"Don't worry, you're not going anywhere. You get to watch as the world worships me." The odd man laughed and again twisted his mustache.

"Why do you do that?"

"Do what?"

"Twist your mustache like that?"

"I'm evil that's what I do." The odd man answered as he held onto his mustache.

"I wasn't aware that evil guys did that."

"Sure, it's right here in the evil guy's hand book." The odd guy produced a book out of thin air that said evil guys handbook on the front.

"I see." Jim shook his head but still didn't understand what was going on.

"You see, I built the machine and as soon as I push that red button, I will be on every tv in the world. People will have no choice but to watch me, then I will hypnotize them and they will worship me." He laughed again as he twisted his mustache. Jim raised an eye brow. "It's in the book. I have to or I'll lose my bad guy's membership card."

"There's a membership?"

"Yes, there is a membership, great benefits. Have you ever seen whiter teeth?" He smiled big for Jim to see.

"So, you really think this is going to work." Jim rolled his eyes.

"Of course, it will work."

"Of course, but what if they just turn their tv off."

The odd man just stood and stared at him for a moment.

"They won't."

"But what if they do?"

"You are not going to foil my plans again."

"Has our hero found a snag in Dick's plan. Can Dick make his plan work? Stay tune and see." A voice came out of nowhere again.

"Of course, I'll make it work." The odd man said

"Who is Dick and where does that voice keep coming from?"

"I'm Dick, Dick Dastardly, and that voice is some announcer guy."

"Wait your name is Dick?" Jim laughed a little.

"Find that funny, do you?" Dick walked up to the cell.

"A little."

"You won't find it so funny when I push the red button and turn this tv on for you to watch me."

"What tv." Just as Jim said it there was a tv in front of him.

Dick laughed and twisted his mustache again and walked over to the red button.

"Are you ready to worship me?" Dick held his pointer finger menacingly over the red button.

"You're not twisting your mustache." Jim pointed out.

"What, oh wait." Dick started twisting his mustache, then went to press the button and back to his mustache, he went back and forth a couple of times, While Jim just rolled his eyes.

"OK, hold on." Dick pulled out his hand book flipped through a couple of pages.

"Ah ha. I only have to twist my mustache when I am laughing evilly. So, I just won't laugh until I push the button first.

Dick looked at Jim who just shrugged his shoulders. Dick pushed the button. A spring sent the red button flying through the air. Springs sprang from every part of the wall.

"Wait what happened." Dick looked confused.

"Looks like your computer broke." Jim smiled as the cage lifted up and he was free.

"But I followed the directions to the letter." Dick was now holding the directions in his hand.

Jim looked closely at the paper. "Where did you get this from?"

"ACME, where I get all my stuff." Dick said sulking.

"I see." Just then there was a tap on Jim's shoulder, He turned to see a coyote standing there.

"Let me introduce myself. I am Wile E. Coyote. Genius. I advised him not to use ACME, but it seems all bad guys get their stuff from there.

"Why Why Why." Dick cried as his dog once again was laughing.

Jim woke in his bed and opened his eyes looking around and sat up slowly.

"You ok honey?" His wife asked.

"Yes, but no more pizza and cartoon network before I go to bed." Jim laid back down.

{ 9 }

The Force

Bruce Santone sat in a small office where there was a large old wooden desk a filing cabinet and two chairs one of which he was sitting on waiting for the captain to come in. He had been hauled in shortly after he shot Joe.

"Dam it Bruce you're not even on the force anymore and you're still causing me trouble." A bald head man screamed at him as he entered the office and slammed the door behind him.

"I can explain."

"It's like you never retired. That's all I ever heard was I can explain."

"Listen this case was the biggest of my career. I worked my ass off to prove what I thought happen. At the time anyway."

"I get that, but again you're not on the force anymore you should have called it in and let us handle it."

"He made me look like an ass and I wanted to bring him in."

"You don't have the authority to do that anymore. Do you know all the questions I'm going to have to answer now?"

"I can make a citizen's arrest."

"You're impossible, I have a man who is supposed to be dead, shot and in the hospital."

"He was going to shoot me. It's all on the tape."

"Yes, a reel to reel, who uses that anymore. We don't have the equipment here to even listen to it."

"And that's my fault?"

"You're missing the point."

"Which is?"

"You're not on the force."

"I'm well aware of that."

"You're retired do some traveling, take up a hobby, sleep in but don't let this happen again." The captain pointed to the door. His bald head red from his blood pressure. Bruce knew that meant the conversation was over. He left the office and everyone scattered as he came out the door, acting like they were not listening.

"I think he misses you." A familiar voice came from behind him.

Bruce turned to see an old friend standing there.

"Well, if it isn't my flat foot friend officer McRoy." McRoy had bright red hair, green eyes and was tall and fit. They shook hands

"Detective McRoy now." He stood back arms open wide to show he wasn't wearing a uniform anymore.

"Well congratulations, it's about time."

"Let's talk. Want to go for some coffee?"

"Yes."

They left the station and headed toward a corner coffee shop.

"I saw your report. I see your mind is still sharp as ever."

"Thank you, but I feel that something is coming that I'm not going to like."

"There are questions as to why you still have all your files. Most files were destroyed when everything was put onto computers."

"Computers they crash you lose everything. Never trusted them."

They entered the coffee shop and order coffee.

"They want those files destroyed."

"And they asked you to do it."

They sat down at a table in the corner.

"Yes."

"So, what do you intend to do?"

"That depends on you."

"What do you mean?"

"I don't have a problem with you having the files, but..."

"But what?"

"Well, if something like this should come up again, I need you to contact me."

"Listen Steve..."

"Now don't get mad."

"I'm not."

"You just called me by my first name, you're mad."

"You..."

"Listen you don't have to contact me officially. Just let me help you so it looks like the department knows what's going on."

"Really?"

"Yes, the captain is going to publicly say that we have destroyed all those old files and that you are retired but were tapped on this because it was your biggest case."

"The captain knows what you're doing?"

"Yes, he isn't happy, but he knows you well enough to know it would be a fight and you probably would have extra copies of some shit as he said it."

"And you're ok with this?"

"Well, I wouldn't do it for just anyone, but for you yes."

"I see."

"Listen the department has been embarrassed, and we are trying not to look bad. Joe has been right under our noses all this time."

"I realize that."

"So?"

"OK, I'm on board."

"Good, because there is more, we need to talk about."

"There is?"

"Yes, Joe has lawyered up already."

"That was fast, but what defense does he have."

"The bigger question is where did the money come from?"

"What do you mean?"

"He is using his old attorney."

"What? That has to cost a fortune."

"Exactly. So where did he get the money?"

"So, who is in charge of the investigation?"

"Officially me. Unofficially us."

"What?"

"The captain knew you would not let this go so he said to work with you. If any questions get raised you are just an advisor since you handled the original case. Your input would be invaluable."

"So, the captain thinks I'm invaluable?" Bruce half smile knowing the truth.

"No, he thinks you are a giant pain in the ass, but he is telling the public that you are invaluable."

They both laughed.

"Ok so what do we know so far?"

"Nothing, you never downloaded your cases onto the computer system and you have the files."

"Computers, can't trust them."

"Yes, but I need to come over to your place and download this case so we have it at the department. Everything has to look on the up and up."

"Ok fine. Come over for a home cooked dinner tonight."

"No, that's ok I have had your cooking before I'll bring dinner."

"My daughter is living with me now. She is a good cook, and about your age I believe."

"Just stop right there. I'm not interested."

"I just made an observation is all. I'll see you around six thirty."

Bruce got up to leave and a young man came up to him.

"Are you Bruce Santone?"

"Yes."

"This is for you." The boy handed him a letter and ran out the door.

"What is it?" Steve was looking over his shoulder.

Bruce opened it and inside was a letter.

"Don't touch it." Steve grabbed it out of his hands.

"I saw it." Bruce said slowly.

They race back to the station and into the forensic office. Then to the captain's office. Where the three waited for results after the captain told them both what a pain in the ass they were. Shortly a young man came into the office.

"Well?" The captain said.

"It was baby powder. But the letter read back off or next time it might be real." The young man said.

"Where there any prints?"

"Just the two of you and I would assume the young boy who gave it to you on the outside. Wiped clean on the inside."

"Well great." The captain glared at the other two. "Seems you are going to be best friends again. McRoy you are now his police protection. Enjoy."

"Wait what?" Steve was confused.

"You have an extra room right Bruce. It's now his. You two are attached at the hip till this is solved."

{ 10 }

The grass is always greener

Allen stood across the street from St. Johns church. His brown hair a dirty mess and his clothes dirty and torn. Tears formed in the corner of his eyes as he watched a young pretty red headed bride enter the church with her equally lovely mother and step father, who would be walking her down the aisle today. He should be doing that, but a series of thinking the grass was greener on the other side had him where he is now.

He started thinking about thirty years or so earlier, high school. He was a senior. He wasn't very popular, mostly his fault. He never kept friends as he always thought hanging out with someone else would be better. His mother often told him he should be happy in the moment, but he was never able to do that. There however was one little red headed girl who never left his thoughts.

"Good morning, Sara." He said as he was getting his books out of his locker.

"Now you're talking to me. Last night I waited for you to call and nothing." She stood looking at him waiting for the lame excuse that was about to come.

"I know you see." He could see in her face that she wasn't going to buy anything he had to say. This was not the first time he had left her hang, but she always came around, for some reason she liked him a lot.

"So, I can expect you to meet me at the diner tonight like we planned." She gave him a look that meant there was only one right answer.

"I'll be there at six." He promised.

He walked into the diner and she was already there waiting for him.

"You made it. Good job." She kissed him on the cheek

His thoughts went to two years later. They had been on again off again. Her parents didn't like him very much as he had hurt her several times and was now back in her life yet again.

"What do you see in him?" Her mother had asked her as she was going out the door to meet him.

"Hi sweety." He kissed her on the cheek

"Let's go." She kissed him back.

"No wait. I know I have messed things up again and again, but I love you."

"I know."

He got down on one knee and pulled out a ring. Her mother came flying out the door as she had been watching from the window.

"Will you marry me. You make me a better man, I need you."

"Allen, oh my God."

Allen put the ring on her finger and she said yes, much to her mother's disappointment. That was the happiest moment of his life.

His thoughts went to his wedding day. He was at the very church he now stood across from. He was alone in a small room and there was a knock on the door.

"Come in."

"Allen, I need to talk to you." Sara's mother said as she closed the door behind her.

She had reluctantly helped her daughter plan her wedding, hoping she would change her mind along the way, but that didn't happen.

"I don't know for sure, but I have a feeling that you have not been faithful to my daughter. She won't listen to reason. I'm telling you right now you are marrying my daughter and that means it's her and her only. Do you get it?"

"Yes."

"Don't forget it either." She turned and left the room.

The wedding went on and they had a daughter a year later. Seeing his daughter being born was the new happiest moment of his life, but a short six months later he was looking at greener grass. A new woman, Brenda, started working at the coffee shop he always stopped at on the way to work.

"Good morning good looking." Brenda said as she gave him is coffee.

"Thank you sexy." He said as he took his coffee.

He looked on the cup and she had written her phone number and a note that said let's have dinner.

His thoughts went to a few weeks later when the baby was having a bad day and Sara was tired and yelled because he was no help at all. He got mad and left and was driving around mad. He looked down and there was the cup with her number on it. He pulled over picked it up. He thought about Sara yelling at him like he was a child.

"I'll teach her a lesson." He called Brenda

"Hi."

"Hey it's Allen."

"Allen, I didn't think you were going to call."

"Want to meet at the diner?"

"What now?"

"Yeah."

"I'll be there in an hour."

"Ok." He hung up and felt bad right away, but he went and met her anyway.

Over the next several months they would meet for dinner and started getting a room to spent more time together. Until one day she had just got out of the shower and heard him on the phone.

"Honey I'll be home soon. Love you to. No, we are almost done with the deck. Ok bye."

She stormed out of the bathroom. "Are you married?"

"Brenda, I thought you were in the shower."

"You're married and cheating with me."

"You don't."

"What understand. You said you lived with your mother. You lied." She was getting dressed quickly.

"You don't understand."

"Oh, I understand. You're a pig. I can't believe I fell for you."

"Please just listen."

She stormed out and didn't answer his call and refused to wait on him at the coffee shop.

A week later he came home from work and Brenda was there talking to Sara. Sara threw him out that night. He slept in his car and missed work the next couple of days and they fired him.

His mother found him just outside of town sleeping in the car, He hadn't showered in days.

"Ok, enough of this. You're going to go back to my house get a shower and then we are going to talk to Sara."

His mom got them into marriage counseling. He moved back in and got his job back. It lasted a couple of years then he found greener grass again, and again his mother helped him get back with her, but five years ago it happened again and this time Sara wanted a divorce and his mother refused to help again. Sara got everything in the divorce and he spent his time drinking and bumming for money.

The yelling across the street got his attention. There was his mother and sister, Her mother and Sara and her new husband. throwing rice at little Rachel as her and her new husband came out of the church.

"The grass is never greener." He said as he sat on the curb behind a car and cried.

{ 11 }

The Thing

It was two thirty when Shawn looked at his watch. He took a big breath and sighed. The frustration clearly showing on his face.

"Late again." He shook his head. "I wonder what 'the thing' will be this time." He said as he walked by a couple of the other waitresses some of which were laughing and some just had a look of disgust on their faces.

"You ok boss man?" One of the waitresses asked

"Just tired of 'the thing'."

"Yeah, several others are to. They have had it with her."

"I know." Shawn patted her on the shoulder and walked on by.

Shawn managed the front end of a small diner the owner was a Greek man who was very nice but tended to give employees more breaks than they deserved. That was the case with this employee Renee.

"Chris." Shawn said as he entered the small office and closed the door. "She is late again."

"Wonder what 'the thing' will be today." Chris laughed.

"Yesterday the thing was her cat got out and she had to catch it." Shawn said

"Isn't she allergic to cats?" Chris laughed

"That's why she doesn't have one." Shawn sighed shaking his head.

"It makes me laugh every time she is late, she always says to you 'see the thing is' whatever story she has made up." Chris laughed again.

"I hate the way she chomps on her gum while she is talking. Like a cow or something."

"Last week didn't she totaled her car twice?"

"You mean the one she drove yesterday that doesn't have a scratch on it. yes, that was the thing last week."

"What about her grandmother being lost at the airport. Wasn't that the thing two weeks ago?"

"Well, she should be here soon. She hasn't called yet so that means only a half hour late."

There was a knock at the office door, and Shawn turned and opened it. It was one of the waitresses.

"She just called she will be in as soon as she can. I'll let her tell you the reason." She smiled and closed the door. As she did you could hear one of the other waitresses say. "You have got to be kidding me." And anther laugh.

"This must be a good one." Shawn moaned. "A call that means more than an hour late."

"You know her grandmother died three months ago when that was the thing." Chris was still laughing.

"What about when the thing was, she had temporary amnesia and forgot what time she was supposed to be here."

"Didn't she have some kind of fake doctors note for that one."

"Yeah, remember it was signed Dr. Seuss"

"Yeah, that's right." Chris was still laughing.

"How about when the thing was, she was going blind."

"And she messed up all those checks."

"Yeah, she owed a lot of money that week for her mistakes."

"But she saw the clock clearly when it was time to leave."

"How many times have you written her up now?" Chris was pulling her file.

"Four, doesn't seem to help."

"Maybe you should write her up again."

"The last time I wrote her up I told her next time she would be fired."

"I don't think I want to do that. She is sweet I hate to see her lose her job."

"I think she needs to go. It is starting to affect the other staff, and morale is dropping."

"I don't know."

"Just let me handle it."

"Ok you handle it, but I hate to see her go."

"Really."

"Yeah, I'll miss the thing." Chris laughed.

"Listen if we are going to let her go today is the day. We are slow so we can run on three girls no problem."

"Yeah, but the thing is…"

"Don't you start with that."

"Do you remember when the thing was, she was allergic to bleach so she couldn't ring out the rags to wipe the tables."

"And we use dawn not bleach in that water, yeah I remember."

"How about when the thing was that ten-car pile-up, she came upon."

"That no one else knew about yeah."

"She is creative."

"She is annoying."

"She should write a book. It could be called 'The thing is.' It would probably be a best seller."

"So, we are letting her go today."

"I'll let you handle it. I'll back you up."

"Thank you."

"Ok the thing is I have to make the soups." Chris got up and left laughing.

Shawn went about his day and an hour and half later Renee strolled in.

"I'm sorry you see the thing is…" Renee was chomping her gum as she talked to Shawn.

"Come in the office with me." Shawn said as he turned and walked not looking to see if she followed or not. They got in the office and he motioned for her to sit at the desk as he closed the door.

"Ok let me have it." Shawn really didn't want to hear it but had no choice.

"You see the thing is there was a big bear sitting at my door and he wouldn't move."

"And."

"Well, I had to wait for him to go."

"You didn't call anyone for help."

"No, I yelled at him through the window."

"Wait don't you live in an apartment building."

"Yes, I know weird isn't it."

"Yes, well here is my thing…." Shawn stopped for a moment realizing what he had said. "I have to let you go. You have shown up late way too many times."

"Wait, you're firing me."

"Yes, I'm sorry. You left me no choice."

"But the thing is, I'm a good worker and…"

"And your always late. Sorry."

Renee got up pushed past Shawn and stormed out of the diner. The other waitresses looked at him shocked.

"The thing is over." Shawn said as he went into the kitchen

{ 12 }

Airplane

Dylan sat looking out the window at the plane he would soon be boarding. He sighed heavily making his brown hair, that hung just above his green eyes, move again. His slender figure sank deep into his chair.

"Relax." The man next to him said patting his leg.

"Gordon, I don't think I should go." Panic showed in Dylan's eyes.

Gordon looked right into his eyes. His green eyes pierced Dylan's soul. He would do anything to make him happy. He knew he wasn't gay, but he was still in love with him.

"All of our friends are waiting for us." Gordon ran his hand through his long red hair pushing it back out of his eyes once again.

Their friends had left a day earlier, but they both had to work so they had to fly out the next morning.

"I just don't..." Dylan stopped and he looked into Gordon's eyes again.

"It will be fine." He smiled big at him and Dylan melted a little.

Dylan let out another deep breath. As far as he knew none of his friends knew he was gay let alone that he was in love with Gordon. He worried that Gordon would not be his friend if he found out, and if a friend was all he was ever going to be he was ok with that.

"Listen take this." Gordon handed him a pill.

"What is it?"

"My dad takes it for anxiety. He said it will help you relax for the flight."

"I don't do meds well." He looked at Gordon's face and quickly took the pill and washed it down with his water against his better judgement.

They sat quietly and soon the announcement came that it was time to board. As Dylan stood up, he felt a little weird. He looked out the window at the plane once more before boarding and all of the sudden it reminded him of a coffin. He grabbed Gordon's arm in a panic.

"It will be fine."

Dylan followed Gordon down the ramp way that seemed like it was closing in around him and just as it seemed like it was going to swallow him, they entered the plane.

"Our seats are right back here." Gordon pointed.

Dylan looked and the arms of the chairs seemed to reach out and try and pull him in. He shook his head trying to clear it.

"Here, you sit by the window." Gordon motioned for him to sit.

He sat and they both buckled up. After what seemed forever, the plane started moving. Moments later, after the safety speech that Dylan didn't really hear much of, the plane was in the air.

"See, not so bad." Gordon said as he padded his knee.

Dylan smiled and closed his eyes for what seemed only minutes.

"What's going on?" Dylan asked as the plane shook. He heard the captain on the speaker but couldn't make out what he was saying.

"It's just turbulence. The captain just said he has to go off course a little to get around a storm." Gordon tried to calm him down. Just then lightning struck an engine and flame shot out of it.

Dylan looked over at Gordon, who was now putting his head between his legs. He reached over and grabbed Dylan by the back of the head and pushed him forward.

"I'm sorry man." Gordon said as the plane shook violently.

People were screaming and then suddenly wind ripped through the plane and they were rushing toward the ground. Without warning water engulfed them.

Dylan felt someone unbuckle him and push him up. Dylan broke the surface of the water and gasp for air.

"Grab your seat." Gordon yelled as he shoved his seat in front of him. They both floated looking around at the broken plane and those who were gone already floating.

"That's blood in the water." Gordon said as he looked around.

"So?" Dylan looked around listening to cries in the distance.

"Sharks. We need to get away from here." Gordon started to kick, and swam away. Dylan realized what he said and followed his lead.

They swam for a while and heard screams. They looked back and saw fins, and they started swimming faster. An hour later they could barely hear the screams anymore and just ahead they saw a beach in the distance.

"Look, we are saved." Gordon pointed.

"I don't think I can…"

"Don't say it. Just keep going."

It took hours but they finally reached the beach. It was dark and they were both exhausted and reluctantly passed out.

Dylan opened his eyes to the sun high in the sky. He went to move, but he was so sore from the events of the past day he wasn't sure he could even move.

"Dylan are you ok?" Gordon said as he sat up.

"I'm alive."

"We have problems."

Dylan opened his eyes again to several guys holding guns on them. The men started to give them orders in another language. Two of them grabbed him and yanked him to his feet.

"Our plane crashed." Gordon pointed to the ocean. The men spun them around slapping cuffs on them as they marched them to an awaiting van.

"What do you think is going to happen?" Dylan asked and the van started moving.

"Well, we are in cuffs, I'm thinking jail."

"If we are going to die...."

"We are not going to die."

"I have something I want to tell you." Dylan's eyes teared up.

"What is it?"

"I'm gay."

"Ok. I don't think that matters now."

"I'm in love with you, I have been for some time."

"I see. I don't know what to say."

"I just wanted you to know is all."

The van came to a stop, and the door opened.

"I guess we are here." Gordon said.

Dylan felt a slap on his face.

"We are here. See I told you it would be fine."

"Wait, what? We didn't crash into the ocean?" Dylan shook his head and opened his eyes.

"We flew from Ohio to Las Vegas. What ocean?" Gordon patted his leg.

Dylan sat quiet as they pulled into the gate.

"So, we are here?" Dylan smiled.

"Yep." Gordon stood and got their bags from the overhead. Dylan slowly stood taking his bag from Gordon who followed him toward the exit. Several people stared at him and he wasn't sure why.

"By the way, you talk in your sleep. Pretty loudly too." Gordon whispered in his ear. Dylan's heart almost stopped. Gordon squeezed his shoulder. "Yes, I know you are gay. We all do and we all know you're in love with me."

Dylan exited the plane, all red faced, wishing it had crashed now.

{ 13 }

Italian Restaurant

Joe sat at a table in a small room, with a small table in front of him. His head was shaved and he had on the orange jump suit he had been wearing everyday for several months now. He had been brough here half hour ago and he wasn't sure why, but felt that Detective Santone was behind it.

"Well Joe Ferella, we have some questions for you." Said a man who was much younger than him. He was dressed in a suit and tie and carried a folder in his hands. Joe just looked at him, not at all intimidated by the strong stance he took standing over him.

"Not without my lawyer."

"You mean the lawyer that Mr. Amato is paying for?"

Joe sat looking at him for a moment.

"I already told the other guy everything, so I don't know what else you want from me."

"How about this?" He laid a paper down in front of him with the lead story being. Santone's Italian Restaurant burnt to the ground. Police investigate.

"I know nothing about this." Joe looked the man in the eyes and shrugged.

"I think you do." The man laid a folder on the table.

"What's in there?" Joe asked trying to hide the nervousness in his voice.

"There is evidence in here that ties you to the fire. Evidence that we have not tied to you because you were supposed to be dead for six months already."

"Then maybe your evidence is wrong."

"Your friend detective Santone suggest we check the finger print we found at the site to yours, and guess what?" The man slammed his hands on the table. "Nothing to say now I see."

"I hate him." Joe mumbled under his breath.

"Do you ever want to see the light of day again?"

"Do you think I'm stupid? I know I'm in here for life. There is nothing you can say that will make me admit to anything." Joe yelled at him, then was immediately mad at himself for getting mad.

"So, you don't want to work with us?" The man paced back and forth in front of him.

"You and I both know you can't cut me any deals."

"Maybe not."

"You know not."

"But everyone knows you are here talking to me today, without your lawyer."

"Yeah, so what?" Joe narrowed his eyes and looked at the man who was now leaning over the table.

"Maybe they find out that you told me everything."

"I told you nothing."

"Mr. Amato has plenty of guys on the inside."

"Are you threating me?"

"No just merely concerned." The man stood and leaned against the wall and folded his arms.

Joe pressed his lips in anger. He had him right where he wanted him. He was left with no choice.

"What do you want?" Joe finally said through his teeth.

"Tell me everything."

"What do I get?"

"I'll make sure you end up in a minimum-security facility. You will have it easy for the rest of your life."

Joe looked at him anger filling his face. "I hate you."

"I don't want to be friends."

"Fine."

"Then start talking." The man sat a tape recorder on the table and started recording.

"It was five months after my death when a man approached me."

* * * *

"You look great for someone who has been dead for five months." A tall slender man smiled at him.

"Listen tell Mr. Amato I'll have the money to him as soon as Santone backs off and I can get to my wife."

"Mr. Amato said he is tired of waiting."

"It's just I didn't plan on Santone to cause so many problems."

"Mr. Amato said, since it's taking so much time you need to do him a favor. Do this favor and he will give you more time."

"And if I don't?"

"I don't think you want me to answer that."

"What is it he wants done?"

"It's nothing really."

"That means it's big."

"There is a business that refuses to work with him anymore."

"And?"

"He wants it taken out. He wants to send a message to others."

"How would I do this?"

"Burn it down."

"What?"

The man produced a set of keys and handed them to him.

"The blue chevy over there has all you will need to do the job. Follow the instructions that are there."

Joe slowly took the keys and looked in the direction the man pointed and saw the car. He looked back and the man was gone.

"Just fucking great." Joe mumbled to himself as he walked to the car. He looked around before unlocking the door and getting in. He looked across to the passenger seat and saw a manilla envelope. He looked around again, then slowly picked it up and opened the envelope.

Good decision Joe, now go to Santone's Italian Restaurant and use the gas in the trunk to set a fire by the back door. Then leave the car at the AMP on the other side of town. Do this and I'll give you two more month to repay me. Fail and well....

Joe flipped the paper around but that was all it read.

"Santone's that's the detective's brother's place." Joe smiled at the thought of causing him some heart break.

For the next two weeks he watched the restaurant to see when the best time to do this would be. He didn't see anything odd going on and wondered why this job needed done. Then one day, the man who had given him this task, was at the restaurant, as he left Mr. Santone was yelling at him.

"I told him I am done. I can't run anymore. Don't come back."

"Run." Joe smiled to himself. "He must have been running some kind of drugs or money laundering for him. Maybe I should just turn him in." Then he remembered the letter. So, the following Thursday evening he set the fire.

* * * *

"That's the whole story?"
"Yes, that's it. I parked the car where they told me to and left."
"So, he only gave you two extra months."
"Yes."
"You never got the money you thought you were going to."
"So."

"What other jobs have you done for him to save your hide."

"Oh no! I'm not telling you anything more. That was not part of the deal."

"I got enough for now." He stopped the recorder. "I'm sure we will be talking again." The man smiled and walked out of the room.

"Don't forget our deal." Joe yelled at him as he left.

Detective Santone popped another circus peanut in his mouth and smiled as he watched from the other side of a two-way mirror.

{ 14 }

Baseball Field

Toby kicked at the dirt at home plate as he held his bat ready to swing. Suddenly he was twelve again and his dad was on the side line yelling at him.

"Wait for a good pitch."

He squinted his eyes and waited for the pitch and swung.

"Strike three." The umpire yelled.

He hung his head and walked back to the dugout.

"It's ok son, next time." His dad patted him on the back as he went to the bench.

"I thought I would find you here." A voice broke in.

"Hey Sandy." Toby was back looking at the empty field. Toby was thirty now and all dreams of being a major league player were gone.

"Dad is asking for you." She said as she stood looking at him with tears in her eyes.

"Why, I've been nothing but a disappointment." Toby swung the bat at nothing.

"I don't think dad sees it that way at all."

"He always wanted me to be a pro player, get married and give him grandchildren."

"He wanted you to be happy, and are you."

Toby dropped the bat, tears in his eyes.

"Steve loves you and is worried about you." She continued.

"I wanted to be everything dad wanted me to be. I wanted him to be proud of me at some point."

"Dad is very proud of you."

"I can't believe this is happening."

"It's hard for all of us."

"I remember like it was yesterday. He coached me in little league."

"Time is short you know."

"What did the doctor say today?"

"They called hospice."

"Then the cancer spread."

"It's in his bones."

He pulled a ball out of his pocket, and held it up.

"This is the ball from the first home run I hit."

"I see."

"He had me sign it for him. He wanted to have this for when I made it to the major leagues."

"That was your dream, dad supported anything we wanted to do."

Her phone went off and she pulled it out of her pocket.

"Who are you texting?"

"Steven, he is worried about you. We all are."

"I'm sorry, I know I should go see him."

"Then let's go."

"It's hard."

"You think it's easy on any of us." She took his hand. "He wants to see you."

He hung his head and followed his sister. They walked the familiar four blocks to their parent's house. Toby's mother hugged him when he walked in.

"He has been asking for you."

"I know."

"They started morphine drip so he isn't totally with it."

Steven hugged him as he walked toward the hallway that led to his parent's bedroom.

"Do you want me to go with you?"

"No, I will be ok. Thank you, baby." He kissed Steven, then laughed a little to himself.

"What is it?" Steven looked confused.

"This is the first time I have kissed you in this house. In front of my mother." Tears rolled from his eyes.

"Are you ok?" Steven took his hand.

"Yes." He let Steven's hand go and went down what seemed to be a much longer hallway than he ever remembered.

"Dad." He said softly as he entered.

"Son, you came." A weak voice came from the shell of a man that Toby remembered.

He walked slowly over to him and his dad lifted his hand and Toby took it in his.

"I want you to know how proud I am of you. I could not have asked for a better son."

"Dad, I know I didn't become what you wanted..."

"Yes, yes you did. You're an honorable man, who is true to himself no matter what. What more could I ask for."

Toby smiled at him. "Thank you, dad."

"Where is that man of yours?"

"He is in the living room."

"Tell him to come in."

Toby thought to argue for a minute but went to the door and yelled for Steven.

"You wanted to see me?" Steven said as he took his outreached hand.

"I may not totally understand everything, but I know love when I see it." He said slowly. He took both of their hands and put them together. "Take care of each other, like your mother and I have. Bless you both." His dad laid back, that little talk took everything he had.

Both men stood, with their tears-stained faces and watched as his father struggled to breathe. Moments later they were in the kitchen telling his sister and mother what had happen.

"I need to go home. I am mentally drained." Toby said as he stood up. They hugged and kissed his sister and mother and went across town to their apartment. They had a quiet dinner and went to bed.

"Honey, wake up." Steven was shaking him.

"What is it?" Toby asked already knowing the answer.

"Your sister just called."

"What time is it?"

"One thirty in the morning."

They just looked at each other, and nothing had to be said as they just hugged and held each other for several moments.

Over the next couple of days Toby spent a lot of time at the ball field. Reliving the best times he had with his dad, and wondering how much strength it took him to tell him those last words. Words that he will never forget.

The day came for the funeral, many friends and family came and he hugged more people that day than he had in his whole life he thought. Steven was right by his side the whole time, and he was proud to have him there. He heard murmurs from family about him and his lifestyle choice. How he hated that word, Choice. Each time he would just think of his dads last words and smile. As long as his parents loved him and were proud of him no one else matter.

The time came when it was just the family left in the room and they walked up to close the casket.

"Thank you, dad. Thank you for understanding even when you don't agree. Thank you for being proud of me." Toby said with Steven standing behind him holding his shoulders.

Toby pulled out the baseball he had signed for his father and looked at his mother who was crying. She pressed her lips and shook her head yes.

"Here dad you will always have the first home run ball of the son you are proud of." He put the ball in the casket by his hand, and with that the casket was closed.

A year later Toby and Steven got married. On a small table, beside the family table, was the picture of Toby and his dad who was holding the home run ball that his son had just signed.

{ 15 }

First Snow Fall

It was late September and the wood sprites were all busy turning the landscape into Autumn. It is after all the job of the wood sprites to bring in each season. Wood sprites, as you may know, are fairy creatures that are only three inches tall with wings, there are millions of these sprites around the world keeping the seasons on track. Tinsel is one such sprite.

"Hey Tinsel wait up." Dash was trying to catch up to him. "What's the hurry?"

"Just trying to get my work done." Tinsel was buzzing around touching green leaves, when he did, they would turn the most beautiful of autumn colors. He and his two friends Dash and Bloom were working in the same part of the forest for several days.

"Did you hear anything yet?" Bloom asked as he joined them.

Tinsel stopped and looked at both of them. His green eyes were lit up like a lighting bug, and he smiled from pointed ear to pointed ear.

"It's your turn isn't it." Dash flew around him then stopped right in front of him.

"Yes." Tinsel said slowly enjoying every second of that short word.

"Oh dude, I'm so happy for you." Bloom was beside Dash now.

"I am so excited. I get to be the one to touch the cloud this year."

One of the highest honors a sprite can have, is to start the first snow fall of the year. One sprite each year touches the snow cloud and release the first snow flake and the first snow fall that follows.

"It's about time. You have asked to do this for ever." Bloom said as they flew down and sat on a small rock in the middle of a creek.

"I know, I have been asking for years. I went to the elders this morning to put my request in, and was told they wanted to see me right away."

"Oh man, you must have lost your mind." Dash shook his head.

"I went in and the three of them just smiled at me and I smiled back."

"Then what?" Dash asked

"One of the elders said it's your time."

"What did you do?" Both of them were ready to burst now.

"I said finally really loud, and they all gave me a look that made me think I just messed everything up."

"But?" Dash said.

"They all smiled and I said thank you and left."

"Which finger are you going to use." Bloom asked

"This one." He held up his pointer finger on his right hand. "Or maybe this one." He held up his pointer finger on his left hand. "I'm not sure yet." He put his hand down.

"So, I heard it's finally your year." A female voice came from behind them. They turned to see Linetta floating on a leaf. She was a friend of sorts, not always the most supportive of friends, but will be there if you're in a jam.

"Yes, it is." Tinsel said proudly.

"Well, I guess it's good for you, you have only wanted to do this for ever."

"Longer I think." Dash said.

"I'll never understand why. I prefer spring, when we bring everything back to life."

"Yes, we know." Bloom said.

"Can you at least be happy for him?" Dash said.

"Not to worry guys nothing can bring me down today. I get to give the children what they look forward to. A chance to catch that first snow flake on their tongue. All because of this finger." He held up his right pointer finger, and looked at it. "Or this one, not sure yet." He held up his left pointer finger.

"You don't even know which finger you're going to use." Linetta said shaking her head and she flew off of the leaf. "Well, I still have leaves to change." She waved and was gone.

"Don't worry about her." Dash waved his hand. "You have a good month or so to decide which finger to use."

"Yeah man, just think about all those kids and how excited they get with the first snow." Bloom said.

"I know. I have always loved the excitement you see in their eyes, and the joy that the first snow brings them." Tinsel flew off the rock.

"Where are you going?" Dash yelled.

"Lots of leaves to change yet before the first snow."

The next month went by slowly for our friend Tinsel. He continued his work bringing autumn in and watched as temperatures slowly dropped. He listened as the children talked more and more about the first snow fall, the excitement in their voices make Tinsel excited as well.

"Well, there he is." Tinsel heard a familiar voice behind him, he turned to see Jack Frost there.

"Hi my friend, I am so happy to see you."

"Yes, I would imagine you are."

"So, you heard the good news."

"Yes, it's your year."

"Yes, and the children seem more excited this year than and I can remember."

"Well, I'm sure you won't let them down."

"No way."

Jack touched the ground and you could see it start to freeze. "Well let me get my job done so you can do yours." Jack smiled at him.

"Thank you, Jack." Tinsel smiled back, as he watched Jack slide off and freeze everything is sight.

Well Tinsel wasn't sure which day the first snow would be, but with Jack in town he knew it would be soon and he was more than ready.

"I will use my right finger, or maybe my left." He said as he flew off.

Ok maybe not one hundred percent ready. But the day soon came and the elders sent for Tinsel. Bloom, Dash and Linetta all stood by to cheer him on. Tinsel flew up to the cloud and looked down at the children, who were looking skyward with anticipation. The excitement in their faces made his heart sing. Tinsel got to the cloud looked down once more and saw the children dancing around and felt their excitement through his whole three-inch body. He looked at both hands, he knew his friends were watching him and cheering but he heard nothing.

Tinsel took his right finger and pushed it into the cloud and the first snow flake of the first snow fall appeared and slowly floated to the earth and landed on a little girl's tongue. She jumped around in delight and she yelled "I caught it." Tinsel pulled his finger back as millions of snow flakes were now falling in the first snow fall of the year. The children were all having a ball laughing, and playing. As for Tinsel well this was the happies moment of his life. One that he would recount with his friends over and over again.

{ 16 }

Ten Dollar Bill

"Well, well take a look at him." Kim said as an all but six feet, beefy, well-built guy with short black hair and a tan walked into the diner. He was wearing a tank top, jeans and work boots. He took as seat at the counter.

"Go ahead Tammy take him. He is your type." Kim pushed Tammy toward him. Kim was slim and short, with short black thick hair and brown eyes.

"Hi sweety what can I do for you?" Tammy asked smiling at him.

"I heard this is a good place for coffee." He smiled at her.

"Pipping hot." She turned and poured him a cup.

"Thank you...."

"I'm Tammy."

"Nice to meet you Tammy I'm Vance." He opened several creamers and poured them in his coffee, then added sugar. Tammy looked over at Kim who nodded for her to keep talking.

"So, your new, I don't think I have ever seen you in here before."

"Yeah, I just moved here from the Philly area."

"That's nice."

"Well, I don't know anything in the area, so kind of board."

"Yeah, I can see that." Tammy nodded.

"She would be glad to show you around." Kim said from the other end of the counter.

He looked at her then at Tammy. "Your wing man."

"Something like that."

Another customer walked in. "Don't worry I got it." Kim said.

"I wouldn't mind if you wanted to show me around. I mean I don't really have any friends here."

"I suppose maybe sometime. I work a lot." Tammy smiled and a bell rang with a yell from the kitchen.

"I have to pick up my food. Nice talking to you, here is your slip for the coffee." She laid his bill down on the counter and went into the kitchen.

Tammy took her food to her table and walked up to the register, where Kim was standing.

"He left already?"

"Yep. Dollar seventy-five for coffee and here is your tip." She dropped a quarter in her hand.

"Really?"

"Sorry."

"He seemed so nice." Tammy said as she picked up his cup to put into a bus pan.

"Wait what's that?" Kim pointed.

It was a ten-dollar bill wrapped around a business card. She unrolled the bill and looked at the card. It said Vance lawn care and services with a phone number and address. She flipped it over and he hand wrote call me on the back.

"Well now this is better." Kim said looking over her shoulders.

"Do you mind." Tammy pulled the card in close to her chest.

"Aww come on, you have to share. I have nothing going on right now."

Tammy laughed and looked at the ten-dollar bill. On the back he wrote trust your wing man.

"See now I like him. He said to trust me."

"Yeah, shows he doesn't know you."

They both laughed and went back to work as several customers came in. A couple days later she called him and they met at a deli for lunch.

"I didn't think you were going to show." He said as he walked her to a small table, and pulled out her chair.

"I don't usually do things like this, but I thought it's a public place what the hell." She half laughed.

"You're just showing me around, not helping me commit a crime." He smiled at her.

"Well to be honest there isn't much to show you."

"To be honest I already knew that."

They both smiled at each for the half. They started talking small talk.

"So, tell me about you."

"Well, I wasn't supposed to live pass five. My heart was underdeveloped, so now I take meds daily to keep me going."

"Why not a transplant?"

"I'm on a list, but I have o negative blood and it's rare and really hard to find a donor."

They made more small talk and went for a walk in the small local park.

"I want to thank you for a nice evening. I hope we can do it again." Vance said as he took her hands.

"I think I would like that." She closed her eyes waiting for the coming kiss, then a horn blew. She opened her eyes to see Vance turning his head away just as he was about to kiss her. There waving honking her horn was Kim.

The next morning when Tammy got to work Kim was already there.

"I saw you took my advice and called him how did it go?"

"It was going fine; he was about to kiss me then some crazy person drove by honking their horn."

"Oh my God. I'm so sorry."

"It's all good. He wants to go out again."

"So that was a date?"

"Didn't start that way, but seem to end that way."

"You have to go out with him. He is a catch. He has his own business."

"I don't know. I'll see."

"You have to. If you don't, you'll be sorry."

"We have customers let's get working."

Over the next several days and weeks they saw a lot of each other and soon were dating.

"Last night was six months." Tammy said gushing as Kim came to work.

"I still hate you. What happen."

Tammy held out her hand and the biggest rock Kim had ever seen sat on her finger.

"OK, now I truly hate you." She grabbed her hand to look closer.

One year later they were married and two years later against doctors' advice she had a baby girl, she named Beverly after her late mother.

Time went by and things were good for them. The pregnancy had taken its toll on her health so she was never able to have any more children, but the one she had was happy and healthy and that's all they wanted.

Twenty-four years into the marriage Tammy's health declined bad. Her heart was struggling and her kidneys were now failing and transplants seemed unlikely. Then one week before their twenty-fifth anniversary Tammy passed away in her sleep. Services were held four days later.

"Hi dad." Beverly said as she walked into the house. Her dad who used to be so full of life sat in his arm chair, as shell of the man he used to be.

"Today is our anniversary." He didn't look up at her at all.

"I know." She handed him an envelope.

"I really don't want a card."

"No, dad. Mom gave me this when she knew she was not going to be here today. She said to give this to you that you would understand."

He looked up at her, his eyes red from crying, to see her tear stain face hold a white envelope that read best tip I ever got. He took it from her, with confusion in his face.

"Open it dad, you will understand."

He opened the envelope and pulled out a ten-dollar bill that read trust your wing man on the back.

{ 17 }

Faded Photograph

"Hi grandma." A young petite, red head girl said as she came in the back door of a small ranch house. An older couple sat at either end of the table. She was sipping coffee and he was reading a newspaper.

"Hey honey, I'm glad you came by." Grandma smiled at her.

"Mom said you wanted to see me." She started to pull a chair out.

"Before you sit down dear will you go in my bedroom and get me the jewelry box off my dresser."

"Ok, grandma." She disappeared down the hallway and was soon back with the box and sat it on the table.

"Sit down here dear." She patted the seat of the chair next to her, and she turned the box toward her.

"What?" The girl looked confused.

"Tara, I want you to look in the box, my eyes a bad, there is a pair of blue sapphire ear rings I want you to have for your wedding."

"Really grandma?" Tara looked surprised.

"Yes honey."

Tara opened the box and looked around the top box.

"I don't see them."

"Take the top out."

She lifted the box out and looked through the things in the bottom.

"These." She pulled out a beautiful pair of blue sapphire ear rings.

"Yes those."

"Oh, grand ma they are beautiful." She laid them down on the table and noticed a faded photograph in the bottom of the box. "What's this." She pulled it out.

"Oh nothing." She took it out of her hand.

"No, really what is it?" She took the pic back.

"Best not to talk about it." She sighed.

"About what?" Grandpa dropped the paper so he could see over it. He saw the picture and gave dirty looks to his wife. "I didn't know you had that." He said and got up and took the paper and went into the living room angry.

"Did I miss something?"

"Well, I might as well tell you now. I forgot I had that picture hid in there."

"Hid?"

"Yes, well that's grandpa and his younger brother."

"I didn't know he had a brother."

"They haven't talked in probably fifty years. He got rid of all the pictures of him and I saved this one. He didn't know I did that."

"Why don't they talk?"

"It's a long story."

"I've got the time."

"It all started when your grandfather turned twenty. He was having a hard time, His dad wanted him to work at the family pizzeria. He wanted to prove he could make it on his own."

"Well, he is stubborn."

"He felt that his parents loved his bother more than him. He wanted to show he could make them proud."

"So, what did he do?"

"He worked in a few other places and ended up at a garage. Not just any garage though. Mr. Marcelo's."

"The mob bosses?"

"The same. He was just pumping fuel at first, but soon he was stealing cars and making big bucks doing it. He was very good and became Mr. Marcelo's favorite."

"I can't believe it."

"Neither could his father when he found out. He told him he had to pick which family he wanted to belong to."

"So, what did he do?"

"He stormed off. He moved into an apartment that Mr. Marcelo got him."

"So that's why his brother won't talk to him?"

"No, it was the start."

"So, then what?"

"Well, a year or more went by, and one day he was standing outside the gas station drinking a soda and his mother walked up."

"I bet he was shocked."

"Well, a little. She told him that his dad was sick, from all the years of smoking. He really wanted him to come home and run the pizzeria with his brother."

"What did he say?"

"At first, he said he couldn't, but then his mother started crying saying how much they worried about him and missed him. How much his brother was lost without him."

"Where were you when all this was going on?"

"We had dated in high school and I kept tabs on him, but we weren't seeing each other at this time."

"So, what did he do?"

"He went to Mr. Marcelo and said he needed to take some time for his family. Mr. Marcelo agreed and gave him two months."

"I'm surprised he agreed to that."

"That's how much he liked him. Anyway, he moved back home and helped at the pizzeria. Things went great him and his brother worked well together. I even agreed to go on a date and we were soon seeing each other again."

"That's good." Tara took her cup and got them both some more coffee.

"Yes, then at the end of two months these two guys showed up. Said Mr. Marcelo said it was time to come back."

"Oh shit."

"Well, he was a little scared, but a week later he went to Mr. Marcelo and said that he wanted out. He was happy being in the family business and had a good girl friend now."

"I bet he was not happy."

"He said he knew to much, and was to much of an asset for him to just let him go."

Tara stirred her coffee shaking her head. "Wow."

"Well, your grandfather got angry and said he was leaving and that was that. He stormed out of the office and left."

"I just can't believe it."

"Well, he went back home and continued to work at the pizzeria. Mr. Marcelo sent men several times to try and talk him into coming back each time he said no. Then one night his men burnt the pizzeria to the ground. It was closed and we think they thought he was there cleaning, but his dad had used his car and was doing some office work."

"Oh my God!"

"The smoke killed him fast, as he was sick from smoking all those years."

"Oh my God!"

"His brother blamed him. Said he never wanted to talk to him again. He never even went to the services. Truth be told he has never forgiven himself. We married a couple years later; his family didn't come even though I invited them. We moved to this side of town."

"Mr. Marcelo never came around again?"

"Like I said he thought he was killed in the fire. He was named after his dad so he saw the name in the paper and either thought it was him or figured he sent the message he wanted to send."

"He has never wanted to try and fix things?"

"Several years ago, his mother passed and I begged him to go to her services, but he didn't. He doesn't think I know that he goes to the grave site from time to time."

"We should find his brother."

"He does think about him a lot. He checks the obituaries every day."

Tara took the picture and looked at it again.

"Wow it's faded but they look a lot alike."

They both looked up to see him walking back into the kitchen tears in his eyes.

"What's wrong grand pa?"

He laid the paper down and pointed to an obituary.

{ 18 }

Ghoast

Samantha sat in her room playing tea party. She had several of her favorite stuffed animals sitting around the small table with her. Her mother walked by and smiled; she loved how much imagination her daughter had.

"You have an empty seat sweety." Her mother pointed out.

"No, I don't."

"Of course, you do, right there." Her mother pointed to the setting right across from her.

"No, my friend is setting there."

"Your friend?"

"What was that. Oh, I see." Samantha said looking at the empty spot. "He said you can't see him." She looked at her mother and smiled.

"I see and what is his name?"

"Joe." Samantha turned and looked at the empty spot again. "Oh I see."

"See what?"

"He said you knew him by Joe Joe."

"He told you that."

"Yes, just now. He is a really nice guy."

Her mother looked like she just saw a ghost and walked away without a word.

Later she was sitting at the kitchen table drinking coffee and her mother walked in.

"What is it dear?"

She pointed to a cup of coffee she had already poured for her. She sat down.

"Mom have you ever talked to Samantha about dad."

"I don't know, why?"

"I don't believe in ghost but the weirdest thing just happened upstairs."

"They are called spirits, Becky darling."

"Whatever, listen Samantha was having one of her tea parties, but she had an empty spot. When I asked why she said her friend Joe was sitting there. Then it was like he talked to her and told her I would know him by Joe Joe."

"Well." Her mother set her cup of coffee down on the table. "That is interesting."

"Not the word I had for it."

"I don't remember ever talking to her about Joe."

"She was only two months old when he passed. There is no way she remembers him."

"Honey this is the old farm house that he grew up in. That's why you bought it. You can stand on the porch and see the house you grew up in. There is a lot of energy around here."

"Mom please don't start you know I don't buy into all that."

"Mommy." Samantha walked into the kitchen.

"Yes, honey."

"Oh, Joe was right. I mean pappy."

"Right about what?" Her mother asked her.

"Joe said, Grammy was here. He told me to come down and tell her something."

"You called him pappy?" Her grandmother asked.

"Yes, he said I could. He looks like a pappy."

"What were you suppose to tell me honey?"

"Um, he said stop using so much sugar, it's better black. I don't understand what he means."

Her mother and grandmother both looked at each other in shock.

"It's ok honey. Go play." Her mother kissed her on the forehead. They both watched her leave the room.

"What is going on?" Her mother shook her head.

"He was telling us it's him. He always yelled at me for using to much sugar in my coffee."

"I know." Becky put her forehead in her hands.

"Why can't you just say there are things that you just don't understand?"

"I don't know. Ghost, spirits whatever they are. It's just all so hard to believe."

"He is watching over you and Samantha. That's a good thing."

"I miss Tom."

"He will be home soon enough. He has a year left in the army, then he will be home."

"Maybe I should tell Samantha not to talk to this Joe."

"Why would you do that?"

"I don't know because it freaks me out. My daughter knows things she shouldn't know. It's weird."

"She is getting a chance to know her grandfather. Why is that so bad?"

"Because he is dead."

"Mommy."

"Yes, dear." Her mother smiled quickly not hearing her walk in.

"Joe said to tell you to stop being shut brained."

"Honey, do you mean close minded?" Her grandmother asked.

"Yeah, that's it." She smiled and bounced off into the living room.

"Joe honey you are not helping." Her mother looked up as she said it.

"Great now you're talking to him."

"Got to admit that's exactly what he would have said if he was here."

"You know what, I think it's bed time."

"Fine, you know best. I'll talk to you tomorrow."

The next several days went by and Samantha talked more about pappy and brought up more things she should not have known.

"Do you want to get a medium and see if he talks to us." Her mother offered.

"I most certainly do not. I talked to Tom, he thinks it's a phase and she will grow out of it."

"I see." She sipped at her coffee.

"Oh, don't give me that disapproving tone."

"I didn't mean anything by it at all."

"I was thinking of maybe taking her to a psychiatrist."

"There is nothing wrong with her. She has a gift."

"She talks to him like he is really there."

"Well to her he is really there."

"That's not normal."

"Who's to say what's normal."

"Why do I try and talk to you."

"I'm going home. I know that tone."

"Good night mother."

"Good night, dear, oh make sure your lock the doors. Tonight, there is some kind of party at the bar down the street. Every year all I hear is drunks all night long."

"OK, mom good night." She locked all the doors then before heading upstairs she double checked the windows then went and put Samantha to bed and went to sleep herself.

In the middle of the night there was pounding on the kitchen door. Becky ran to the top of the steps. Samantha came out of her room.

"Get back in your room honey." Becky motioned to her.

"Tina, I know you're in there." A drunk voice yelled at the top of his lungs.

"You have the wrong house." Becky said as she came down the stairs.

"Tina come out now." The man continued to yell.

Becky dialed 911 just as the man broke the window with a stone.

"Come out now."

"911 please hold for the next available operator."

"You have got to be kidding me." She yelled into the phone.

"Tell her to come out now." The man yelled again and he threw himself into the door and she could hear it crack under his weight. Another hit or two and he would be in. Then suddenly she heard a loud crash and saw dust outside the door.

"911 what's your emergency?" Came a voice on the phone.

"There is a drunk man trying to break into my house."

"I am sending help. Find a safe place till they get there."

"Ok." She said slowly.

Ten minutes later the police arrived and arrested him.

"I can't believe what happen." She was telling her mother the next morning over coffee.

"So, the top of the chimney fell off and knocked him out cold."

"The cops said thank God that happen. This guy had a history of violence and would have hurt me, not realizing he was at the wrong house."

"You had this place inspected before you bought it didn't you?"

"The chimney is only a couple years old."

"I see."

They both heard a noise and looked to the kitchen door and jumped. They could barely make out the shape of a man standing there.

"I will always protect my family." A whisper of a familiar voice said and the man was gone.

They looked at each other with tears.

"I give, I believe. Thank you, dad."

{ 19 }

Blue Sky

"Thank you, Cathy. No, he will be fine. Ok I will bring him up Saturday. Thanks again this helps a lot." Debbie hung up the phone and looked at her son, Terry, who just turned and ran down the hall to his room.

Debbie hung her head. Terry had said he didn't want to go to his Aunt Cathy's for the summer, but she was left with no real choice. They lived in Philadelphia and the apartment building they lived in was sold and going to be torn down. Dave, her husband got a promotion at the bank and they couldn't leave and they were having a hard time finding a place. Which meant that they would have to stay in a hotel and put things in storage until they found a place.

"Honey, you know with both of us working we can't leave you alone in a hotel." She said standing in his door way. He had buried himself under his blankets.

"I don't want to go."

"Your cousin Ryan is your age the two of you will have a good time."

"I have friends here."

"Honey, you play games online with them. You can do that there."

"They live in the middle of nowhere, they probably don't have internet."

"Honey, don't you think we are going to miss you?"

"Then why send me?" He sat up in his bed and pulled the blankets off his head.

"You know why. We have been through this a hundred times. We tried to find a place in time, but there just isn't anything we can afford. We have to move."

"I can stay at the hotel by myself. I'll be very quiet."

"A ten-year-old boy alone in a hotel. This isn't home alone and you could get hurt." She went and sat on the bed beside him, pulled back her long brown hair that fell in her face.

"But mom."

"No but's baby. It breaks my heart to not have you with me, but Aunt Cathy is the best option. I need you to be a big boy, pack up what you want to take. I'm taking you there in two days." She looked him in the eyes and he knew that was the end of the conversation and he lost.

"OK." he hung his head went to his closet and pulled out his spiderman suitcase.

"That's my boy. It will go by fast, and when you come back your new room will be all ready for you."

Two days went by super-fast for Terry. His dad had given him a big hug that morning and said how proud of him he was. That didn't make him feel any better.

Four hours later after several pit stops; they reached his aunt Cathy's house. It was somewhere call Juniata County. The closest town was Richfield. Terry couldn't believe how small the town was.

"I don't think I am going to like this. There will be nothing to do here."

"You will find plenty to do."

"Look I have no service on my phone."

His mother looked at him and smiled as they pulled into a dirt drive way. They drove for a couple of minutes and a big white farm house appeared. His mother parked the car and looked at Terry.

"It will be ok."

"I doubt it." He said under his breath.

They got out of the car as a lady, with black curly hair, came off the porch and hugged his mother.

"It's so good to see you." She said as she hugged her.

"I know. We are sisters we shouldn't spend so much time apart."

"I know, but I have the farm, and you with your work."

"I really appreciate this. We are in a real pickle."

"Not a problem, he will fit right in I am sure."

Terry stood there looking around thinking to himself. Not likely.

"I would love to stay, but there is so much to do. The movers are coming Monday at eight am."

"I understand. Don't worry I will take good care of Terry."

"Now you be good for your Aunt Cathy."

"I will mom."

She kissed him on the top of his head and he watched as she backed up and then drove out the drive way. His aunt was standing there waving at her.

"Now come Terry. It's been a long time. I think you were only four when you were here last." She put her hand on his shoulder and walked him into the house.

Yes, and thankfully I don't remember it. He thought to himself and smiled at her.

He was not happy when he realized he was sharing a room with his cousin Ryan. That was going to make it harder to just hide from everyone. Ryan had tried to get him to play outside and go on the four-wheeler, but Terry just hung out in the bedroom unless he was eating.

"Mom he is weird. He doesn't want to do anything." Terry overheard Ryan telling his mom one night when he was on the way down the stairs for dinner.

"He isn't weird. He is lonely. He misses his mom, dad, and all his friends. If you had to go stay with him you would be the same way."

"I don't think I would like living in a big city."

"He feels the same about living here."

"You think he will go to dutch days with us."

"That's up to him."

Terry walked into the kitchen and they stopped talking.

"Hi honey, you ok?"

"Yes, thank you."

"Dinner will be ready shortly."

"You want to go play on the swings out back." Ryan asked hopefully.

Terry thought to say no, but then thought about the weird comment. "Yes, please."

Ryan looked shocked and looked at his mother.

"Don't get too dirty, dinner will be soon." Neither boy was sure what to do, but for different reasons. "Well, be off with you."

They both ran outside, Terry followed Ryan to the swings. Neither said anything right away. Terry was surprised how good it felt to have fun.

"What is dutch days?" Terry said after a few minutes.

Ryan looked at him not sure what to say. That was probably the most Terry had said to him in the three weeks he had been there.

"It's the small fair in town. It's in a couple of weeks. They have games and really good food."

Terry smiled and he decided in that moment he should try to have fun, even if his mom and dad weren't there.

"Are those the four wheelers over there?" Terry pointed.

"Yeah."

"You still want to take me out on them."

"I would love to." Ryan smiled big now.

"Cool, can we do it tomorrow?"

"Yeah, I'll get my friend Joel to go with us. He is a little older than us and mom likes when he is along. She said she feels safer that way."

"Boys dinner."

They ran into the house all smiles.

"I see some fresh air did wonders." She smiled at them as they ate, and exchanged glances with her husband.

The next morning Joel came over and Aunt Cathy packed them some snacks and thanked Joel for taking them. They road on dirt paths. Terry road with Joel since he had never road a four-wheeler before. They stopped at the edge of a field an hour later. Terry took his helmet off and looked around in amazement.

"There is a creek over that way that we go swimming in." Ryan looked at Terry. "Is something wrong?"

"No, I just don't think I ever saw a sky so blue in my life. It's so clear out here, and smell so good."

"Are the skies not blue in Philly?" Ryan was confused.

"There are buildings everywhere, sometimes it's hard to see the sky. This is so beautiful."

They rode the rest of that morning and early afternoon they got home.

"So did we have fun?"

"More than I thought possible." Terry said.

She looked at Ryan who shrugged his shoulders. That night Ryan showed Terry how to catch lighting bugs, and Terry was just as amazed by the stars in the sky as he was by the blue sky. He went to Dutch days and enjoyed every minute he could. When his mother came to pick him up, he asked to come back again next summer.

{ 20 }

Central Park

"Mom." Sammy yelled as she came in the front door, followed by her teen-aged daughter.

"She is in the kitchen dear." Her father said from behind the news paper he was reading, while sitting in his favorite chair.

"Thanks dad."

"Hi grand pa." The teenage girl waved as she went by. He marveled at her, how much she looked like her mother at that age, and they both looked like his beautiful wife. He smiled at the thought, and kept on reading.

"I got the ticket for Rent." Sammy announced as she entered the kitchen.

"Oh, I don't know, your dad won't go." She pushed her lips together and shook her head.

"I know I talked to him yesterday. So, the two of us are going to take you."

"Yeah grandma, it will be fun."

"I have always wanted to go to New York." She thought for a moment.

"Mom already bought the tickets." Her granddaughter made a puppy dog face.

"Tom, honey do you mind..."

"Go, have fun. I'll have some peace and quiet around here." He laughed.

"OK, when do we leave?"

"I'll pick you up Friday morning, I rented a nice car for the trip."

"That's in two days."

"Yep, so get packing grand ma."

Friday morning came quick and Sammy was there to pick her up bright and early.

"Now do you have everything you need." She asked Tom for the hundredth time.

"Yes, dear now go and have fun. Maybe I'll go do some fishing or something."

"Don't be stinking up the kitchen with fish."

"Would you go."

"You know it feels weird doing something without you."

"I know, but you have always wanted to see a Broadway show. So please go have fun."

"Ok, mom your bags are loaded. You do know we will be home Monday."

"I know, I just didn't know what to bring."

"Ok, dad love you. Don't worry we will take good care of her."

They all got into the car and Tom waved with a big smile on his face as they drove off.

"So, what is the plan, what are we doing?" Her mother asked as they got onto the interstate."

"Well, it's about a six-hour drive, we will stop on the way and grab a bite to eat. We check into the Hilton this afternoon and I figured we would hit time square tonight."

"Sounds good to me." Her mother was all smiles. She had always wanted to see New York and with only weeks till Christmas it would be all lit up. She felt like a little girl again.

They got to New York and went through the Lincoln tunnel.

"I can't believe all this traffic. So many people, I don't think I have ever seen this many people in my life."

Her daughter and grand daughter just smiled at her. They had both been to the city before and loved it.

"Ok mom, this is the hotel." Sammy pulled into a parking garage.

"This seems very fancy dear. I hope this isn't costing you too much."

"it's fine mom." She smiled at her.

They checked in and came back down stairs. Sammy got a cab, her mother thought she was going to get hit.

"Why aren't we driving the rented car?"

"Not in the city mom. Parking is a nightmare. Cabs are much easier."

They took the cab to time square and walked around checking out the shops.

"It's all lit up so beautifully. I have never seen anything like it." She looked around amazed.

They went in and checked out shops and got coffees.

"I can't believe the price of a coffee." She looked at the size of the cup. "I'll drink is slow and make it last."

"Mom it's alright. Whatever you want."

After a couple hours of going from shop to shop. Getting a trinket here and there, they were tired.

"Can we just go back to the room, I'm tired."

"Yes of course mom."

Once back at the hotel, they all showered and ordered food.

"What are we doing in the morning?"

"Well, the show isn't till Sunday, so I thought maybe central park would be nice."

"Oh, I've read a lot about that place. I can't wait to see it." Her mother smiled and then the smile left her face.

"What's wrong mom?"

"Oh, nothing. Central Park it is." She smiled again.

"Good morning mom."

"Where did you go. I woke up and no one was here."

"I got you breakfast." She sat a sandwich and coffee on the table for her.

"Oh, thank you dear." She ate in quiet.

"Is something wrong mom?"

"Nothing dear, just trying to take in everything from yesterday."

"So, you're enjoying yourself gram?"

"Oh, yes, my dear. It's a dream come true thank you so much."

"After the park do you want to go the Statue of Liberty?"

"Maybe. I'm old you know I tire easily." She laughed.

"Well, then let's head to the park. It's a nice brisk morning, but not too cold today."

"Well, let's go." They all bundled up and soon were at the park entrance.

"What is it mom?" Sammy asked as her mother stared off at something in the distance.

"The horse drawn carriages. I love them."

"Then let's walk over and check them out gram." She took her hand and they started walking. They got to them and Sammy looked at her.

"Are you ok mom?" She noticed tears in her eyes.

"Your father had always promised that if we ever made it to New York, he would take me on one of these."

"Really?"

"Yes, when we married, we had no money really and I had said it would have been beautiful to have been in one to go to the reception."

"He said...."

"Honey if we ever get to New York I'll take you on one through central park."

She looked in the carriage to see who cut her off and Tom was sitting there waiting for her.

"Your carriage awaits you my beautiful bride."

"But," She looked back at her daughter and granddaughter, who were smiling from ear to ear.

"I can't believe you all did this." She said crying as Tom helped her into the carriage, and they snuggled under a blanket as they slowly rode through Central Park making her dream come true.

Tom spent the rest of the weekend with them, went to the show and all the other sites, but for her the carriage ride will always be the best part of her life.

{ 21 }

About the Author

Donald L Murray Jr. was born in central Pennsylvania. As a senior in high school, Donald wrote his first book, a Hardy boy's style book, that got him an A in English class. Donald spent four years in the Army, where he lived in Germany, as well as being involved in the first gulf war. Since coming home, he moved to northeast Pennsylvania where Donald was involved with community theater for over twelve years as well as taking an improve class in New York City. Donald married his husband, Anthony, and took his last name, Marino. Besides sitting at home writing Donald also loves to travel. Donald's favorite author is Terry Brooks.

www.ingramcontent.com/pod-product-compliance
Lightning Source LLC
LaVergne TN
LVHW012053070526
838201LV00083B/4517